GO!
with Microsoft®

Internet Explorer 10
Getting Started

D0140776

GO!

with Microsoft®

Internet Explorer 10

Getting Started

**Shelley Gaskin and
Heddy Pritchard**

Boston   Columbus   Indianapolis   New York   San Francisco   Upper Saddle River
Amsterdam   Cape Town   Dubai   London   Madrid   Milan   Munich   Paris   Montréal   Toronto
Delhi   Mexico City   São Paulo   Sydney   Hong Kong   Seoul   Singapore   Taipei   Tokyo

Editor in Chief: Michael Payne
Executive Acquisitions Editor: Jenifer Niles
Editorial Project Manager: Carly Prakapas
Product Development Manager: Laura Burgess
Development Editor: Ginny Munroe
Editorial Assistant: Andra Skaalrud
Director of Marketing: Maggie Leen
Marketing Manager: Brad Forrester
Marketing Coordinator: Susan Osterlitz
Managing Editor: Camille Trentacoste
Senior Production Project Manager: Rhonda Aversa

Operations Specialist: Maura Zaldivar-Garcia
Senior Art Director: Jonathan Boylan
Cover Photo: © photobar/Fotolia
Associate Director of Design: Blair Brown
Director of Media Development: Taylor Ragan
Media Project Manager, Production: John Cassar/Renata Butera
Full-Service Project Management: PreMediaGlobal
Composition: PreMediaGlobal
Printer/Binder: RR Donnelley
Cover Printer: Lehigh-Phoenix Color/Hagerstown
Text Font: MinionPro

10 9 8 7 6 5 4 3 2

ISBN 10: 0-13-314583-2
ISBN 13: 978-0-13-314583-0

Table of Contents

Internet Explorer 10

Chapter 1 Using Internet Explorer 10 to Explore the World Wide Web 1

About the Authors

Shelley Gaskin, Series Editor, is a professor in the Business and Computer Technology Division at Pasadena City College in Pasadena, California. She holds a bachelor's degree in Business Administration from Robert Morris College (Pennsylvania), a master's degree in Business from Northern Illinois University, and a doctorate in Adult and Community Education from Ball State University (Indiana). Before joining Pasadena City College, she spent 12 years in the computer industry, where she was a systems analyst, sales representative, and director of Customer Education with Unisys Corporation. She also worked for Ernst & Young on the development of large systems applications for their clients. She has written and developed training materials for custom systems applications in both the public and private sector, and has also written and edited numerous computer application textbooks.

This book is dedicated to my students, who inspire me every day.

Heddy Pritchard is an adjunct professor in the School of Engineering and Technology (EnTec) at Miami Dade College and in the School of Office Careers/Computer Science/Computer Science-Industrial at Broward College. She holds a bachelor's degree in Computer Information Systems from Florida Atlantic University and a master's degree in Computer Information Systems from Nova Southeastern University (Florida). She has been a programmer/analyst for 26+ years and involved in the development of numerous applications.

This book is dedicated to students who want to improve their lives with the use of computers.

GO! with Internet Explorer 10

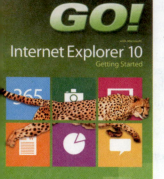

GO! with Internet Explorer 10 is the right solution for you and your students in today's fast-moving, mobile environment. The GO! Series content focuses on the real-world job skills students need to succeed in the workforce. They learn to use Internet Explorer 10 by working step-by-step through practical job-related projects that put the core functionality of Internet Explorer 10 in context. And as has always been true of the GO! Series, students learn the important concepts when they need them, and they never get lost in instruction, because the GO! Series uses Microsoft procedural syntax. Students learn how and learn why—at the teachable moment.

What's New

New Design reflects the look of Windows 8 and Office 2013 and enhances readability.

Enhanced Chapter Opener now includes a deeper introduction to the A & B instructional projects and more highly defined chapter Objectives and Learning Outcomes.

New GO! Learn It Online Section at the end of the chapter indicates where various student learning activities can be found, including multiple choice and matching activities.

New Styles for In-Text Boxed Content: Another Way, Notes, More Knowledge, Alerts, and **new *By Touch* instructions** are included in line with the instruction and not in the margins so that the student is more likely to read this information.

New Visual Summary focuses on the four key concepts to remember from each chapter.

New Review and Assessment Guide summarizes the end-of-chapter assessments for a quick overview of the different types and levels of assignments and assessments for each chapter.

New End-of-Chapter Key Term Glossary with Definitions for each chapter.

A Microsoft® Office textbook designed for student success!

- **Project-Based –** Students learn by creating projects that they will use in the real world.

- **Microsoft Procedural Syntax –** Steps are written to put students in the right place at the right time.

- **Teachable Moment –** Expository text is woven into the steps—at the moment students need to know it—not chunked together in a block of text that will go unread.

- **Sequential pagination –** students have actual page numbers instead of confusing letters and abbreviations.

Student Outcomes and Learning Objectives – Objectives are clustered around projects that result in student outcomes.

New Design – Provides a more visually appealing and concise display of important content.

Scenario – Each chapter opens with a job-related scenario that sets the stage for the projects the student will create.

Project Activities – A project summary stated clearly and quickly.

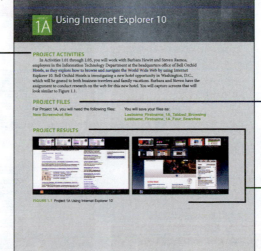

Project Files – Clearly show students which files are needed for the project and the names they will use to save their documents.

Project Results – Show students what successful completion looks like.

In-Text Features
Another Way, Notes, *More* Knowledge, Alerts, and By Touch Instructions

Microsoft Procedural Syntax – Steps are written to put the student at the right place at the right time.

Color Coding – Each chapter has two instructional projects, which is less overwhelming f or students than one large chapter project. The two projects are differentiated by different colored numbering and headings.

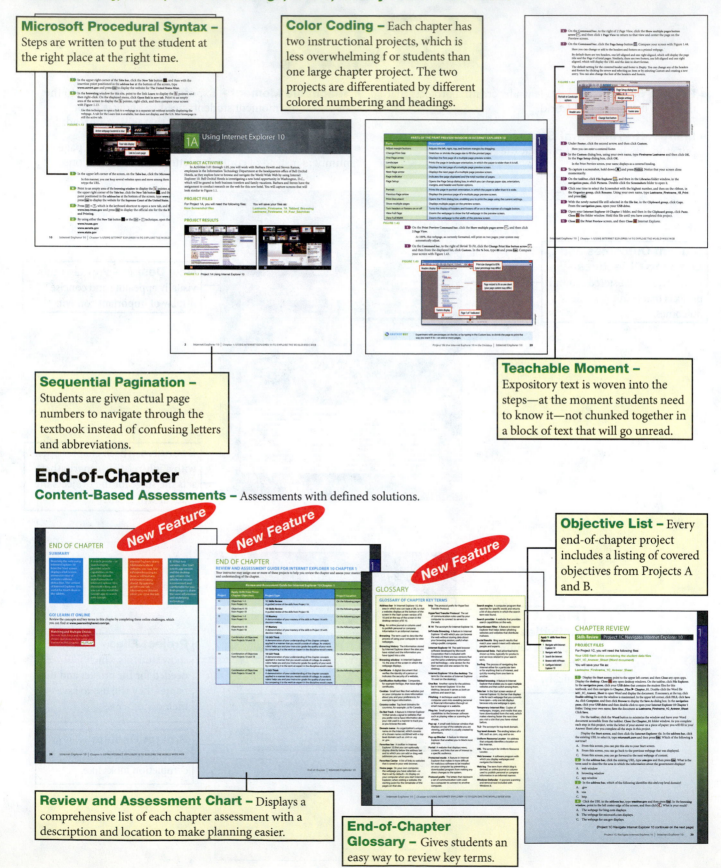

Sequential Pagination – Students are given actual page numbers to navigate through the textbook instead of confusing letters and abbreviations.

Teachable Moment – Expository text is woven into the steps—at the moment students need to know it—not chunked together in a block of text that will go unread.

End-of-Chapter
Content-Based Assessments – Assessments with defined solutions.

New Feature

Objective List – Every end-of-chapter project includes a listing of covered objectives from Projects A and B.

Review and Assessment Chart – Displays a comprehensive list of each chapter assessment with a description and location to make planning easier.

End-of-Chapter Glossary – Gives students an easy way to review key terms.

End-of-Chapter

Content-Based Assessments – Assessments with defined solutions. (continued)

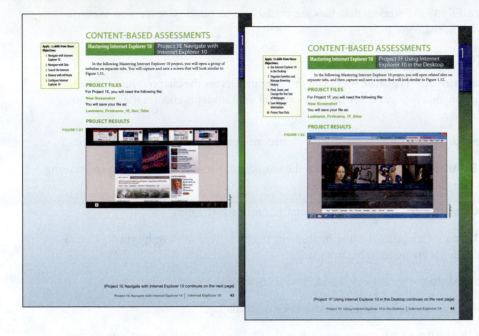

End-of-Chapter

Outcomes-Based Assessments – Assessments with open-ended solutions.

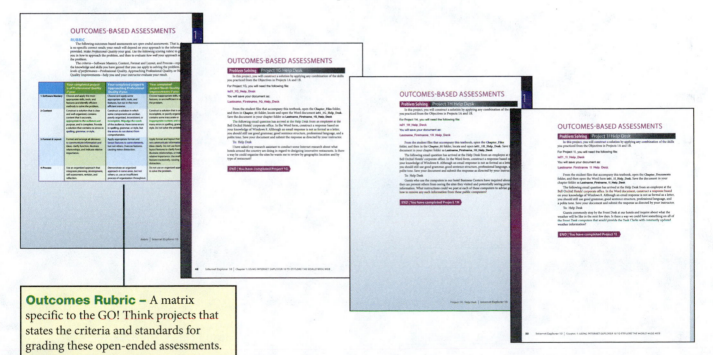

Outcomes Rubric – A matrix specific to the GO! Think projects that states the criteria and standards for grading these open-ended assessments.

Student Materials

Student Data Files – All student data files are available to all on the Companion Website: www.pearsonhighered.com/go.

Instructor Materials

All Instructor and Student materials available at pearsonhighered .com/go

Student Assignment Tracker – Lists all the assignments for the chapter. Just add the course information, due dates, and points. Providing these to students ensures they will know what is due and when.

Scripted Lectures – A script to guide your classroom lecture of each instructional project.

Annotated Solution Files – Coupled with the scorecards, these create a grading and scoring system that makes grading easy and efficient.

PowerPoint Lectures – PowerPoint presentations for each chapter.

Scoring Rubrics – Can be used either by students to check their work or by you as a quick check-off for the items that need to be corrected.

Syllabus Templates – For 8-week, 12-week, and 16-week courses.

Test Bank – Includes a variety of test questions for each chapter.

Companion Website – Online content such as the Online Chapter Review, Glossary, and Student Data Files are all at www.pearsonhighered.com/go.

Reviewers

GO! Focus Group Participants

Kenneth Mayer	Heald College
Carolyn Borne	Louisiana State University
Toribio Matamoros	Miami Dade College
Lynn Keane	University of South Carolina
Terri Hayes	Broward College
Michelle Carter	Paradise Valley Community College

GO! Reviewers

Abul Sheikh	Abraham Baldwin Agricultural College
John Percy	Atlantic Cape Community College
Janette Hicks	Binghamton University
Shannon Ogden	Black River Technical College
Karen May	Blinn College
Susan Fry	Boise State University
Chigurupati Rani	Borough of Manhattan Community College / CUNY
Ellen Glazer	Broward College
Kate LeGrand	Broward College
Mike Puopolo	Bunker Hill Community College
Nicole Lytle-Kosola	California State University, San Bernardino
Nisheeth Agrawal	Calhoun Community College
Pedro Diaz-Gomez	Cameron
Linda Friedel	Central Arizona College
Gregg Smith	Central Community College
Norm Cregger	Central Michigan University
Lisa LaCaria	Central Piedmont Community College
Steve Siedschlag	Chaffey College
Terri Helfand	Chaffey College
Susan Mills	Chambersburg
Mandy Reininger	Chemeketa Community College
Connie Crossley	Cincinnati State Technical and Community College
Marjorie Deutsch	City University of New York - Queensborough Community College
Mary Ann Zlotow	College of DuPage
Christine Bohnsak	College of Lake County
Gertrude Brier	College of Staten Island
Sharon Brown	College of The Albemarle
Terry Rigsby	Columbia College
Vicki Brooks	Columbia College
Donald Hames	Delgado Community College
Kristen King	Eastern Kentucky University
Kathie Richer	Edmonds Community College
Gary Smith	Elmhurst College
Wendi Kappersw	Embry-Riddle Aeronautical University
Nancy Woolridge	Fullerton College
Abigail Miller	Gateway Community & Technical College
Deep Ramanayake	Gateway Community & Technical College
Gwen White	Gateway Community & Technical College
Debbie Glinert	Gloria K School
Dana Smith	Golf Academy of America
Mary Locke	Greenville Technical College
Diane Marie Roselli	Harrisburg Area Community College
Linda Arnold	Harrisburg Area Community College - Lebanon
Daniel Schoedel	Harrisburg Area Community College - York Campus
Ken Mayer	Heald College
Xiaodong Qiao	Heald College
Donna Lamprecht	Hopkinsville Community College
Kristen Lancaster	Hopkinsville Community College
Johnny Hurley	Iowa Lakes Community College
Linda Halverson	Iowa Lakes Community College
Sarah Kilgo	Isothermal Community College
Chris DeGeare	Jefferson College
David McNair	Jefferson College
Diane Santurri	Johnson & Wales University
Roland Sparks	Johnson & Wales University
Ram Raghuraman	Joliet Junior College
Eduardo Suniga	Lansing Community College
Kenneth A. Hyatt	Lone Star College - Kingwood
Glenn Gray	Lone Star College - North Harris
Gene Carbonaro	Long Beach City College
Betty Pearman	Los Medanos College
Diane Kosharek	Madison College
Peter Meggison	Massasoit Community College
George Gabb	Miami Dade College
Lennie Alice Cooper	Miami Dade College
Richard Mabjish	Miami Dade College
Victor Giol	Miami Dade College
John Meir	Midlands Technical College
Greg Pauley	Moberly Area Community College
Catherine Glod	Mohawk Valley Community College
Robert Huyck	Mohawk Valley Community College
Kevin Engellant	Montana Western
Philip Lee	Nashville State Community College
Ruth Neal	Navarro College
Sharron Jordan	Navarro College
Richard Dale	New Mexico State University
Lori Townsend	Niagara County Community College
Judson Curry	North Park University
Mary Zegarski	Northampton Community College
Neal Stenlund	Northern Virginia Community College
Michael Goeken	Northwest Vista College
Mary Beth Tarver	Northwestern State University
Amy Rutledge	Oakland University
Marcia Braddock	Okefenokee Technical College
Richard Stocke	Oklahoma State University - OKC
Jane Stam	Onondaga Community College
Mike Michaelson	Palomar College
Kungwen (Dave) Chu	Purdue University Calumet
Wendy Ford	City University of New York - Queensborough Community College
Lewis Hall	Riverside City College
Karen Acree	San Juan College
Tim Ellis	Schoolcraft College
Dan Combellick	Scottsdale Community College
Pat Serrano	Scottsdale Community College
Rose Hendrickson	Sheridan College
Kit Carson	South Georgia College
Rebecca Futch	South Georgia State College
Brad Hagy	Southern Illinois University Carbondale
Mimi Spain	Southern Maine Community College
David Parker	Southern Oregon University
Madeline Baugher	Southwestern Oklahoma State University
Brian Holbert	St. Johns River State College
Bunny Howard	St. Johns River State College
Stephanie Cook	State College of Florida
Sharon Wavle	Tompkins Cortland Community College
George Fiori	Tri-County Technical College
Steve St. John	Tulsa Community College
Karen Thessing	University of Central Arkansas
Richard McMahon	University of Houston - Downtown
Shohreh Hashemi	University of Houston - Downtown
Donna Petty	Wallace Community College
Julia Bell	Walters State Community College
Ruby Kowaney	West Los Angeles College
Casey Thompson	Wiregrass Georgia Technical College
DeAnnia Clements	Wiregrass Georgia Technical College

Using Internet Explorer 10 to Explore the World Wide Web

PROJECT 1A

OUTCOMES
Use Internet Explorer to navigate and search the World Wide Web efficiently.

OBJECTIVES

1. Navigate with Internet Explorer 10
2. Navigate with Tabs
3. Search the Internet
4. Browse with InPrivate
5. Configure Internet Explorer 10

PROJECT 1B

OUTCOMES
Use Internet Explorer in the Desktop to navigate and search the World Wide Web efficiently.

OBJECTIVES

6. Use Internet Explorer 10 in the Desktop
7. Organize Favorites and Manage Browsing History
8. Print, Zoom, and Change the Text Size of Webpages
9. Save Webpage Information
10. Protect Your Data

Sergey Nivens/Fotolia

In This Chapter

In this chapter, you will browse the web using Internet Explorer 10. When using Internet Explorer from the Windows 8 Start screen, you will see how the experience is optimized for touch and for distraction-free browsing. Browsing the web is one of most common activities of computer users. You will use tabbed browsing, in which you can open multiple websites while researching a project. Internet Explorer 10 also includes features to make printing and saving webpages easy. You will also pin Favorites to the Start screen for instant access and notifications. Finally, you will learn how to keep your web browsing safe and private.

The projects in this chapter relate to the **Bell Orchid Hotels**, headquartered in Boston, which owns and operates resorts and business-oriented hotels. Resort properties are located in popular destinations, including Honolulu, Orlando, San Diego, and Santa Barbara. The resorts offer deluxe accommodations and a wide array of dining options. Other Bell Orchid hotels are located in major business centers and offer the latest technology in their meeting facilities. Bell Orchid offers extensive educational opportunities for employees. The company plans to open new properties and update existing properties over the next decade.

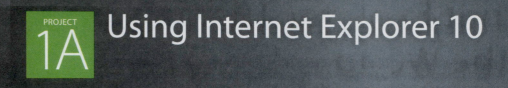

PROJECT 1A

Using Internet Explorer 10

PROJECT ACTIVITIES

In Activities 1.01 through 1.05, you will work with Barbara Hewitt and Steven Ramos, employees in the Information Technology Department at the headquarters office of Bell Orchid Hotels, as they explore how to browse and navigate the World Wide Web by using Internet Explorer 10. Bell Orchid Hotels is investigating a new hotel opportunity in Washington, D.C., which will be geared to both business travelers and family vacations. Barbara and Steven have the assignment to conduct research on the web for this new hotel. You will capture screens that will look similar to Figure 1.1.

PROJECT FILES

For Project 1A, you will need the following files:

New Screenshot files

You will save your files as:

Lastname_Firstname_1A_Tabbed_Browsing
Lastname_Firstname_1A_Four_Searches

PROJECT RESULTS

FIGURE 1.1 Project 1A Using Internet Explorer 10

Objective 1   Navigate with Internet Explorer 10

A *web browser* is a software program that you use to display webpages and navigate the Internet. *Internet Explorer 10*—also referred to as *IE 10*—is the web browser software developed by Microsoft Corporation and that is included with Windows 8.

When launched from the Windows 8 Start screen by clicking the Internet Explorer tile, the browser displays in the full-screen, immersive view like other Windows 8 apps—no distracting windows or toolbars or menus display. IE 10 is built with a touchscreen interface but works equally well with a keyboard and mouse.

Browsing is the term used to describe the process of using your computer to view webpages. *Surfing* refers to the process of navigating the Internet either for a particular item or for anything that is of interest, and then quickly moving from one item to another.

Browsing the web is one of the most common activities performed by individuals who use computers. Common tasks that you perform on the Internet might include looking at your favorite news sites, managing your finances with your bank, conducting research, shopping, sending email messages, using social media sites such as Facebook or Twitter, or reading or writing entries in a *blog*. A blog—short for *web log*—is an online journal or column used to publish personal or company information in an informal manner. For example, the developers of Microsoft Word maintain a blog of information about using Word at http://blogs.office.com/b/microsoft-word/

Activity 1.01   Navigating with Internet Explorer 10

1 Display your **Start screen**, and then compare your screen with Figure 1.2.

If you have been using Windows 8 on your computer, your Start screen will differ. For purposes of this instruction, just be sure you can see the Internet Explorer tile.

FIGURE 1.2

If your Internet Explorer tile is missing, it is probable that a another browser, such as Chrome, is set as the default browser. If your Internet Explorer tile displays a small e in the lower left corner instead of a large e centered in the tile, the desktop version of IE 10 has been set as the default.

To return the Start screen version of IE 10 as the default, follow these steps: On the Start screen, type default programs and then press ENTER to display the Default Programs dialog box. Click Set your default programs, and then on the list, click Internet Explorer. Click OK to close the dialog box.

2 On the **Start screen**, click the **Internet Explorer** tile, and notice the **address bar** at the bottom of the screen.

The *address bar* displays at the bottom of the screen where you can type the address of the website you want to visit, or you can type a search term. Buttons for various tools display on the right. The website that displays will vary, depending on whether you have set a home page or if you have visited a webpage and then closed Internet Explorer 10. The default site is Microsoft's MSN site—yours may differ.

Because Internet Explorer 10 is optimized for a touchscreen experience, the address bar displays at the bottom of the screen where it is easy to use and reach when using touch gestures.

The address bar displays when you open a webpage and reappears when you right-click or swipe up from the bottom of the screen.

3 Point to the bottom of the screen, click the existing web address—the URL—to select it, type **bing.com** and then click or tap **Go** ⊙ or press ⏎. Compare your screen with Figure 1.3, and then take a moment to study the table in Figure 1.4.

URL is the acronym for *Uniform Resource Locator*, which is an address that uniquely identifies a location on the Internet.

On most webpages, you can click links to other webpages. For example, the Bing site displays links to trending information and other news items.

FIGURE 1.3

- Browsing window
- Photo image will differ from this one shown
- Forward button
- Page tools/App available button
- Back button
- Site icon
- Pin site button
- URL typed in address bar
- Refresh button

FIGURE 1.4

PARTS OF THE INTERNET EXPLORER SCREEN	
Screen Part	**Description**
Browsing window	Displays the webpage content for the site you are visiting.
Address bar	Provides the area in which you type the URL for the site you want to visit, and which also works as a search box; also provides buttons for tools and navigation.
Back button	Displays the previous page you visited; activates after you visit more than one webpage.
Site icon	Displays the icon of the website currently displayed in the browsing window; the Internet Explorer icon displays if IE 10 detects no icon for the site.
Refresh button	Reloads the webpage you are viewing to see updates since the last time you viewed it.
Pin site button	Displays a command to pin the current webpage to the Start screen.
Page tools/App available button	Displays a menu to search on the current webpage or to view the same page on the Internet Explorer desktop application. A + on the button indicates that this site has an app available, which you can install from the menu.
Forward button	Displays the next page if you used the Back button.

4 ▸ In the **address bar**, click to select the existing URL, and then compare your screen with Figure 1.5.

When you click the existing URL in the address bar, Internet Explorer 10 may display websites that you visit frequently, websites that you have selected as Favorites, or websites that you have pinned to the Start screen.

FIGURE 1.5

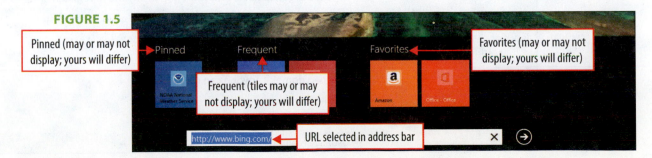

- Pinned (may or may not display; yours will differ)
- Frequent (tiles may or may not display; yours will differ)
- Favorites (may or may not display; yours will differ)
- URL selected in address bar

5 With the current URL selected, type **www.usa.gov** and press [Enter]. Compare your screen with Figure 1.6.

As you type in the address bar, Internet Explorer 10 will use its autocomplete feature to assist you in reaching sites that you visited previously, are Pinned or Favorites, or are popular URLs. The tiles for these sites may also display, and you can click or tap the tile to access the website. Or, as soon as the complete URL is visible, you can press [Enter] or click or tap the **Go** button ⊙.

Because of the Windows 8 roaming feature, you will be able to access recent webpages on all of your PCs.

FIGURE 1.6

USA.gov

The website for the U.S. Government displays. By typing in the address bar and pressing [Enter], the new URL opens.

A URL contains the ***protocol prefix***—in this instance ***http***—which stands for ***HyperText Transfer Protocol***. HTTP represents the set of communication rules used by your computer to connect to servers on the web. Internet Explorer defaults to the *http* prefix, so it is not necessary to type it, even though it is part of the URL for this site.

The protocol prefix is followed by a colon and the separators //.

A URL also contains the ***domain name***—in this instance *www.usa.gov*. A domain name is an organization's unique name on the Internet, and consists of a chosen name combined with a ***top level domain*** such as *.com* or *.org* or *.gov*. ***TLD*** is the acronym for top level domain.

A L E R T !	**Websites Update Content Frequently**

As you progress through the projects in this chapter, the pictures of various websites may not match your screens exactly, because website administrators frequently update content. This will not affect your ability to complete the projects successfully.

---

6 Take a moment to study the table in Figure 1.7 to become familiar with top level domains.

There are two types of top level domains—the generic top level domains, such as .com, .org, and so on, and the ***country codes*** such as .ca for Canada, .cn for China, and .uk for United Kingdom.

FIGURE 1.7

COMMON DOMAIN NAME EXTENSIONS AND ORGANIZATION TYPES	
Domain Name Extension	**Organization Type**
.com	Commercial businesses and companies.
.net	Formerly for Internet service providers and other communications-oriented organizations, but now open to anyone to register.
.org	Usually nonprofit organizations, but open to anyone to register.
.edu	U.S. educational only.
.gov	U.S. government only.
.info	An open domain; anyone can register.
.mobi	Mobile devices.
.name	Individuals and families.
.biz	Usually small businesses.

7 ▷ Point to the bottom of the screen, click the URL text to select it, type **weather.gov** and then press Enter to display the website for the **National Weather Service**.

8 ▷ In the **address bar**, on the left, click the **Back** button 🔙 one time.

The Back button takes you to the previous page you visited, and is active after you visit more than one webpage.

9 ▷ In the **address bar**, on the right, click the **Forward** button ➡ to move to the next page—the **National Weather Service** website.

Recall that the Forward button takes you to the next page if you used the Back button.

10 ▷ In the **address bar**, click the URL text to select it, type **abcnews.com** and then press Enter. On the **Page tools** button ⚙, notice that a + displays on the button. Click **Page tools** ⚙ to display a menu, and then compare your screen with Figure 1.8.

A + on the Page tools button indicates that this site has an app available, which you can install by clicking the button and then on the menu, choosing *Get app for this site*.

An app is useful for sites that you want to explore and navigate without using a browser. Especially on a touch device, apps enable you to enjoy the experience without using a lot of navigation buttons.

FIGURE 1.8

Menu displays
Get app for this site
Find on page
View on the desktop

+ on Page tools button indicates an app is available

http://abcnews.go.com/

More Knowledge **Using Flip Ahead**

On a touchscreen device, the *flip ahead* feature enables you to swipe across the page to move to the next page of content. This is especially useful in news sites that support flip ahead; for example the Windows 8 News and Finance apps. Flip ahead is usually enabled by default. To check your system to be sure this feature is enabled, from the browsing window, display the charms, click the Settings charm, and then click Internet Options.

---

11 ▷ Click the **Back** button 🔙 one time to return to the website for the **National Weather Service**, and then on the **address bar**, click **Pin site** 📌. On the displayed menu, click **Pin to Start**, and then compare your screen with Figure 1.9.

The logo and name for the National Weather Service display.

FIGURE 1.9

Menu displays logo and name for site

NOAA National Weather Service

AA National Weather Service

Pin to Start

Pin site button

http://www.weather.gov/

National Weather Service

12 ▷ Click **Pin to Start** to pin this site to your **Start screen**.

13 ▷ In the **address bar**, click the URL text to select it, and then type **office.microsoft.com** and press Enter.

14 Move your pointer up about half way on the screen and away from the **address bar**, and then point to the left edge of the screen to display the **Back** button ◄ in the **browsing window**. Compare your screen with Figure 1.10.

The area of the screen that displays the contents of the website is the *browsing window*. When you point to the left edge of the screen, a Back button ◄ displays. You can click the button, or by touch, use a flick gesture to go back to the previous page.

15 If necessary, point to the left edge of the screen again to display the **Back** button ◄, and then click the button to go back to the **National Weather Service** website.

BY TOUCH   Flick the Back button ◄ to the right.

16 Point to the center right side of the **browsing** window, click the **Forward** button ▶ one time to display the next page—the **Microsoft Office** page.

BY TOUCH   Flick the Forward button ▶ to the left.

17 Point to the top of the screen to display the 🖐 icon, and then drag to the bottom of the screen to close Internet Explorer 10 and redisplay the **Start screen**.

More Knowledge	**Two Ways to Redisplay the Address Bar**

After a webpage displays for a while, the address bar is no longer visible. Two keyboard shortcuts can redisplay only the address bar without the Tabs bar—Alt + D or Ctrl + L.

Objective 2   Navigate with Tabs

Tabbed browsing is a feature in Internet Explorer that enables you to open multiple websites and then switch among them. In this activity, you will work with Barbara and Steven, who are conducting research on the new hotel in Washington, D.C.

Activity 1.02   Navigating with Tabs

1 From your **Start screen**, click the **Internet Explorer** tile.

The displayed website will be your home page if one is set or the last webpage you displayed before closing Internet Explorer.

2 Click in the **address bar** to select the existing URL, type **microsoft.com** and then press Enter.

3 ▶ Point to an empty area of the **browsing window** until the 🔯 pointer displays, and then right-click to display the **Tabs bar** and the **address bar**. Compare your screen with Figure 1.11.

Use this right-click technique anytime you want to redisplay the address bar.

At the top of the screen, the *Tabs bar* displays a tile for each webpage that you currently have open—only one tab displays because only one webpage is open. The address bar displays at the bottom of the screen.

Unless you open a website in a new tab, each site you open replaces the previous site that was open. At the right side of the Tabs bar, the New Tab and Tab tools buttons display. Use the New Tab button to open a website in a new tab. Use the Tab tools button to manage tabs.

FIGURE 1.11

🔄 **ANOTHER WAY**   Press ⊞ + Z to display the Tabs bar and the address bar.

🔄 **BY TOUCH**   Swipe down from the top of the screen to display the Tabs bar and the address bar.

4 ▶ On the right side of the **Tabs bar**, click the **New Tab** button ⊕, and notice that the insertion point displays at the bottom of the screen ready for you to type a new URL or search term.

5 ▶ Type **www.whitehouse.gov** and press Enter to display the official website for the **The White House**.

As you type, recall that Internet Explorer 10 will use autocomplete to suggest sites you have visited, favorite or pinned sites, or sites that IE 10 recognizes as a popular site.

6 ▶ Point to an empty area of the **browsing** window to display the 🔯 pointer, hold down ⊞ and press Z. Compare your screen with Figure 1.12.

At the top of the screen, the Tabs bar displays tiles for the previous webpage you had open—the Microsoft site—and the current site, which is bordered in blue.

FIGURE 1.12

Current tab bordered in blue

Two tabs display

www.whitehouse.gov

ALERT! **The Right-Click Technique May Not Display the Tabs Bar and Address Bar on Some Websites**

For some websites, the right-click technique may not display the Tabs bar and address bar because the site may not be updated for newer browser techniques. You can use the keyboard shortcut [⊞] + [Z] instead.

7 ▸ In the upper right corner of the **Tabs bar**, click the **New Tab** button ⊕, and then with the insertion point positioned in the **address bar** at the bottom of the screen, type **www.usmint.gov** and press [Enter] to display the website for **The United States Mint**.

8 ▸ In the **browsing** window for this site, point to the link **Learn** to display the 👆 pointer, and then right-click. On the displayed menu, click **Open link in new tab**. Point to an empty area of the screen to display the ▷ pointer, right-click, and then compare your screen with Figure 1.13.

Use this technique to open a link to a webpage in a separate tab without actually displaying the webpage. A tab for the Learn link is available, but does not display, and the U.S. Mint homepage is still the active tab.

FIGURE 1.13

Active webpage bordered in blue

Four tabs display

Link to Learn page

New tab for Learn link created but not displayed

www.usmint.gov

9 ▸ In the upper left corner of the screen, on the **Tabs bar**, click the **Microsoft Home Page tab**.

In this manner, you can keep several websites open and move among them without having to retype the URL.

10 ▸ Point to an empty area of the **browsing window** to display the ▷ pointer, and then right-click. In the upper right corner of the **Tabs bar**, click the **New Tab button** ⊕, and then with the insertion point positioned in the **address bar** at the bottom of the screen, type **www.supremecourt.gov** and press [Enter] to display the website for the **Supreme Court of the United States**.

11 ▸ Press [Ctrl] + [T], which is the keyboard shortcut to open a new tab, and then type **www.bep.treas.gov** and press [Enter] to display the official site for the **the Bureau of Engraving and Printing**.

12 ▸ By using either the **New Tab** button ⊕ or the [Ctrl] + [T] technique, open the following three sites.
www.house.gov
www.senate.gov
www.state.gov

13 ▸ Point to an empty area of the **browsing window** to display the ▨ pointer, right-click to display the **Tabs bar**, and then compare your screen with Figure 1.14.

Depending on your screen resolution, the tabs will display on one or two rows.

FIGURE 1.14

Nine tabs display (your row arrangement may differ)

Tab for house.gov

Tab for the U.S. Senate

Tab for U.S. Department of State

Browsing window (updated content will display different from this figure)

www.state.gov

14 ▸ In the **Tabs bar**, locate the tile for the **The White House**, and then in the upper right corner of the tile, click **Close Tab** ⊗. Compare your screen with Figure 1.15.

Use this technique to close a single tab.

FIGURE 1.15

Eight tabs display; The White House tab closed

Your row arrangement may differ

www.state.gov

15 ▸ To capture a screenshot of your **Tabs bar**, hold down ⊞ and press PrintScrn. Notice that your screen dims momentarily.

16 ▸ Press ⊞ to display the **Start screen**, and then locate and click the **File Explorer** tile. If you do not see your File Explorer tile, with the Start screen displayed, type **file explorer** and then click the app to start it.

17 ▸ In the **Libraries** folder window, in the **navigation pane**, click **Pictures**. Double-click the **Screenshots** folder to open it.

18 ▸ Click one time to select the Screenshot with the highest number, and then on the ribbon, in the **Organize group**, click **Rename**. Using your own name, type **Lastname_Firstname_1A_Tabbed_Browsing** and press Enter.

19 ▸ With the newly named file still selected in the **file list**, in the **Clipboard group**, click **Copy**. From the **navigation pane**, open your **USB drive**, and then in the **New group**, click **New folder**. Name the folder **Internet Explorer 10 Chapter 1**

20 Open your **Internet Explorer 10 Chapter 1** folder, and then in the **Clipboard group**, click **Paste**. Hold this file until you have completed this project.

21 **Close** ❌ the folder window, and then press ⊞ to redisplay the **Start screen**.

22 Click the **Internet Explorer** tile, and notice that your tabs still display.

Because you did not close the app, all of your tabs and the current webpage remain active.

23 In the **Tabs bar**, click the **Tabs tool** button ☺, and then click **Close tabs**.

Each open tab closes, and only the active webpage displays in the Tabs bar.

24 Point to the top of the screen to display the ✋ pointer, and then drag it to the bottom of the screen to close the **Internet Explorer** app.

Objective 3 Search the Internet

The Internet can connect you to a vast amount of information, but first you have to find the information that you need. From Internet Explorer 10, you can search by typing a search term directly into the Address bar.

Activity 1.03 | Searching the Internet

A **search provider**—also called a **search engine**—is a website that provides search capabilities on the web. The default search provider in Internet Explorer is Microsoft's Bing. To search with Google, you can download and install the Google app from the Windows Store.

1 Display your **Start screen**. Point to the upper left corner of your screen, and then move the mouse downward slightly to see if any apps are open; **Close** any open apps.

2 Click the **Internet Explorer** tile.

3 Click in the **Address bar** to select the existing URL, type the search term **"washington dc tourism"** and then press Enter. Compare your screen with Figure 1.16.

On the left, Bing displays suggested related links to websites, and in the list of results, words in your search term *washington dc tourism* display in bold.

In the center, Bing displays **sponsored links**—paid advertisements shown as links, typically for products and services related to your search term. Sponsored links are the way that search sites like Bing, Google, and others earn revenue.

On the right, Bing displays **Social Results**. Bing matches your search intent with relevant people and experts and displays them here.

For example, if you are planning a trip to San Francisco, friends in your social network who live in or have traveled to San Francisco might display if you are signed into Facebook. In addition, experts in the field might display.

Placing quotation marks around your search term limits the search results to only those webpages that contain the exact phrase that you typed.

FIGURE 1.16

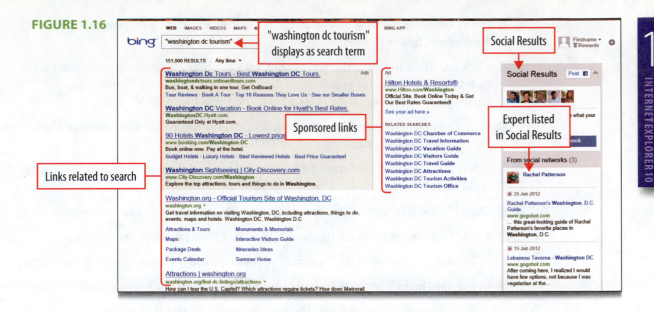

4 ▶ Point to an empty area of the screen to display the ▧ pointer, and then right-click to display the **Tabs bar**. Click the **New Tab button** ⊕, and then in **address bar** type **washington dc hotels** and press ⌷Enter⌷.

5 ▶ Press ⌷Ctrl⌷ + ⌷T⌷ to open a new tab, and then in the **address bar**, search for "**washington dc memorials**"

6 ▶ Press ⌷Ctrl⌷ + ⌷T⌷ to open a new tab, and then in the **address bar**, type **find washington dc chamber of commerce** and then press ⌷Enter⌷. Compare your screen with Figure 1.17.

FIGURE 1.17

7 ▶ Point to an empty area of the screen to display the ▧ pointer, and then right-click to display the **Tabs bar**. Compare your screen with Figure 1.18.

Four tabs with your four searches display. Use this technique when you are searching for multiple search terms to gather information so that you can switch among the sites you have targeted.

FIGURE 1.18

8 ▶ To capture a screenshot of your **Tabs bar**, hold down ⌷⊞⌷ and press ⌷PrintScrn⌷. Notice that your screen dims momentarily.

9 ▶ Press ⌷⊞⌷ to display the **Start screen**, and then locate and click the **File Explorer** tile. If you do not see your File Explorer tile, with the Start screen displayed, type **file explorer** and then click the app to start it.

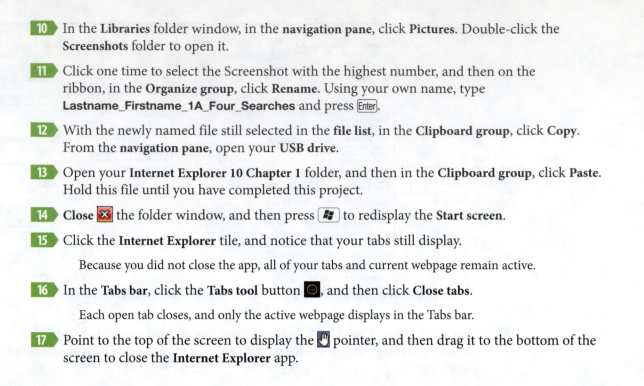

10 ▶ In the **Libraries** folder window, in the **navigation pane**, click **Pictures**. Double-click the **Screenshots** folder to open it.

11 ▶ Click one time to select the Screenshot with the highest number, and then on the ribbon, in the **Organize group**, click **Rename**. Using your own name, type **Lastname_Firstname_1A_Four_Searches** and press Enter.

12 ▶ With the newly named file still selected in the **file list**, in the **Clipboard group**, click **Copy**. From the **navigation pane**, open your **USB drive**.

13 ▶ Open your **Internet Explorer 10 Chapter 1** folder, and then in the **Clipboard group**, click **Paste**. Hold this file until you have completed this project.

14 ▶ **Close** ❎ the folder window, and then press 🪟 to redisplay the **Start screen**.

15 ▶ Click the **Internet Explorer** tile, and notice that your tabs still display.

Because you did not close the app, all of your tabs and current webpage remain active.

16 ▶ In the **Tabs bar**, click the **Tabs tool** button ⚫, and then click **Close tabs**.

Each open tab closes, and only the active webpage displays in the Tabs bar.

17 ▶ Point to the top of the screen to display the 🖑 pointer, and then drag it to the bottom of the screen to close the **Internet Explorer** app.

NOTE | **Printing a Webpage**

To print a webpage, with the webpage displayed, press Ctrl + P to display the Print pane on the right. Click the printer, adjust your settings, and then click Print.

Objective 4 | Browse with InPrivate

As you browse the web, Internet Explorer stores information about the websites you visit. It also stores information that you are frequently asked to provide. For example, if you type your name and address into a website, Internet Explorer stores that information. All of this information is referred to as your *browsing history*.

Usually it is useful to have this information stored on your computer, because it speeds your web browsing and might automatically provide information so that you do not have to type it over and over.

Internet Explorer stores the following types of information:

- *Temporary Internet files*, which are copies of webpages, images, and media that you have downloaded from the web. Storing this information makes viewing faster the next time you visit a site that you have visited before.

- *Cookies*, which is the term used to refer to small text files that websites put on your computer to store information about you and your preferences, for example login information.

- A history of websites that you have visited.

- Information that you have entered into websites or the address bar, including your name and address if you have entered it into a site, and the URLs that you have visited before.

- Saved web passwords.

Activity 1.04 | Using InPrivate Browsing

Use *InPrivate Browsing* to browse the web without storing data about your browsing session. This feature is useful because it prevents anyone else who might be using your computer from seeing what sites you visited. By opening an InPrivate tab, websites that you visit in that tab along with passwords you enter, cookies you create, and temporary files that are downloaded are all deleted when you close the tab or close Internet Explorer.

Use this feature if you are browsing on a public computer, such as in your college labs or at a public library.

1 Display your **Start screen**. Point to the upper left corner of your screen, and then move the mouse downward slightly to see if any apps are open; **Close** any open apps.

2 Click the **Internet Explorer** tile, point to an empty area of the screen to display the ⊿ pointer, and then right-click to display the **Tabs bar** at the top of the screen.

3 On the right side to the **Tabs bar**, click the **Tab tools** button ⊙, and then click **New InPrivate tab**. Compare your screen with Figure 1.19.

> A message indicates that InPrivate is turned on, and in the address bar, a blue icon indicates InPrivate. In this way, you know that your online activity is not being stored by the browser software.

FIGURE 1.19

4 In the **address bar**, type **www.si.edu** and press Enter to display the home page for the Smithsonian.

5 Click in the **address bar** to select the URL you just typed, and then type **www.gwu.edu/varsity-sports** Notice that InPrivate browsing is still in effect, and then press Enter.

> While using InPrivate Browsing, Internet Explorer stores some information. For example, cookies are kept in memory so pages work properly, but are cleared when you close the browser window. Temporary Internet files are also stored so pages work properly, but are deleted when you close the browser window. Webpage history, form data, and passwords are not stored at all.

6 Point to the top of the screen to display the 🖑 pointer, and then drag it to the bottom of the screen to close the **Internet Explorer** app.

> Cookies are cleared and temporary files are discarded.

From the Settings pane, you can configure Internet Options for Internet Explorer 10.

Activity 1.05 | Configuring Internet Explorer 10

 Display your **Start screen**, and then click the **Internet Explorer** tile.

 Point to the upper right corner of your screen to display the **charms**, and then click the **Settings** charm. Compare your screen with Figure 1.20.

FIGURE 1.20

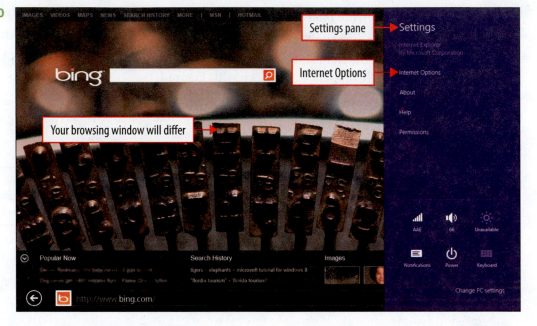

 In the **Settings pane**, click **Internet Options**, and then compare your screen with Figure 1.21.

To delete your browsing history, temporary files, cookies, and saved passwords, under Delete Browsing History, you can click Delete.

Under Permissions, you can decide whether or not you want a webpage that you visit to ask for your physical location. Because many people now use Internet Explorer from a mobile device—a smartphone, tablet, or laptop—more webpages are asking for your physical location when you visit them. Sometimes this is useful to get local information, sometimes the website wants to send you local advertising.

The default Zoom level is 100%. Depending on your screen's resolution, the size of your screen, and your own preferences, you can set the level as low as 60% or as high as 260%.

Flip ahead is usually disabled by default, so you can enable it here. This feature is useful for sites that return multiple pages of information—for example, Bing, eBay, Trip Advisor, and most news sites. The feature enables you to swipe in from the right edge of the screen by touch to view the next page.

The last setting is Encoding, which you will need only if you are visiting a website where the text is not displaying properly. This can occur with websites in other languages.

FIGURE 1.21

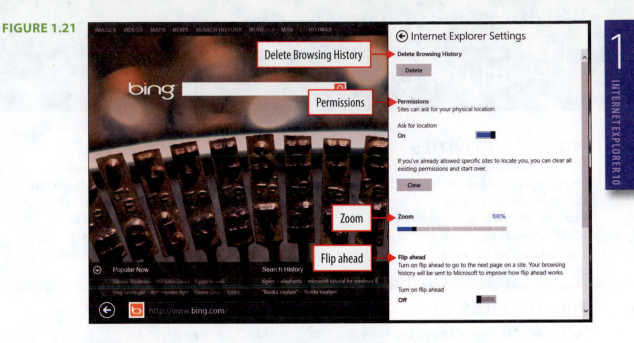

4. In the upper left corner of the **Internet Explorer Settings pane**, click the **Back** button 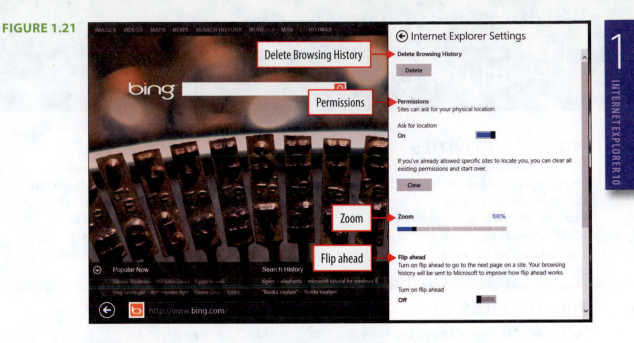 to close the pane.

5. Point to the top of the screen to display the pointer, and then drag it to the bottom of the screen to close the **Internet Explorer** app.

END | You have completed Project 1A

PROJECT ACTIVITIES

In Activities 1.06 through 1.16, you will work with Barbara Hewitt and Steven Ramos, employees in the Information Technology Department at the headquarters office of Bell Orchid Hotels, as they explore how to browse and navigate the World Wide Web by using Internet Explorer 10 in the desktop. Bell Orchid Hotels is investigating a new hotel opportunity in Washington, D.C., which will be geared to both business travelers and family vacations. Barbara and Steven have the assignment to conduct research on the web for this new hotel. You will capture screens that will look similar to Figure 1.22.

PROJECT FILES

For Project 1B, you will need the following files:

New Screenshot files

You will save your files as:

Lastname_Firstname_1B_Open_Tabs
Lastname_Firstname_1B_Favorites
Lastname_Firstname_1B_Print

PROJECT RESULTS

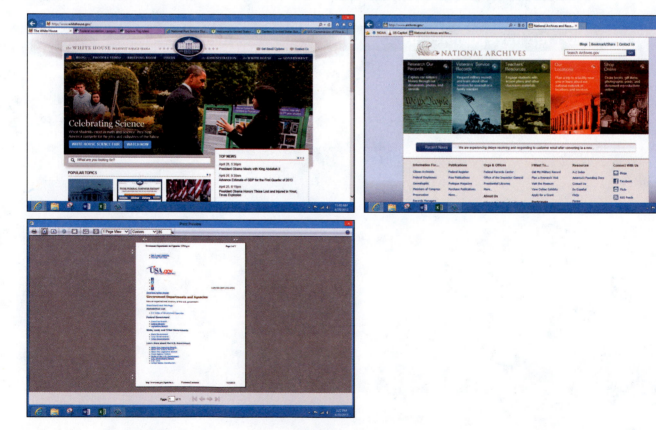

FIGURE 1.22 Project 1B Use Internet Explorer 10 in the Desktop

Recall that the desktop is the area in Windows 8 where you use desktop apps. In Windows 8, there are two versions of Internet Explorer 10—the touch-friendly immersive version that you practiced from the Start screen and the desktop version referred to as *Internet Explorer in the desktop*. Both use the same underlying technologies, and both demonstrate quick startup, reliable performance, and adherence to the highest levels of web standards.

Internet Explorer 10 in the desktop has an additional feature. It can run *plug-ins*, which are small programs that add capabilities to the browser such as playing video or scanning for viruses. In the Start screen version of Internet Explorer 10, the plug-in for Adobe Flash is built into the browser so that you can view videos such as those on YouTube. No other plug-ins can be added to the Start screen version of Internet Explorer 10.

The decision as to which version of Internet Explorer 10 you use will depend on your device and your own preferences. On a touchscreen device such as a tablet, you will probably prefer to use the touch-friendly version from the Start screen. If you spend most of your time using desktop apps with a mouse and keyboard, such as Microsoft Office, you will probably prefer to use Internet Explorer 10 in the desktop.

Activity 1.06 | Using Tabbed Browsing with Internet Explorer 10 in the Desktop

1 Display your **desktop**, **Close** ☒ any open windows, and then on the taskbar, click **Internet Explorer** 🅮. Compare your screen with Figure 1.23, and then take a moment to study the table in Figure 1.24 that describes the parts of the Internet Explorer window.

If you have not set a home page, the default is Microsoft's msn.com news site. Here Microsoft's site is shown as the home page.

On your computer, home page refers to whatever webpage you have selected—or is set by default—to display on your computer when you start Internet Explorer. When visiting a website, home page refers to the starting point for the remainder of the pages on that site.

For example, your computer manufacturer may have set its company site as the default home page. At your college, the home page of your college's website might be the home page on the computer at which you are working.

FIGURE 1.23

FIGURE 1.24

PARTS OF THE INTERNET EXPLORER IN THE DESKTOP SCREEN	
Screen Part	Description
Back button	Displays the previous page you visited; activates after you visit more than one webpage.
Forward button	Displays the next page if you used the Back button.
Site icon	Displays the icon of the website currently displayed in the browsing window; the Internet Explorer icon displays if IE 10 detects no icon for the site.
Address bar (also called the One Box)	Provides the area in which you type the URL for the site you want to visit, and which also works as a search box.
Page tab	Displays the name of the active webpage.
New Tab button	Opens a new tab.
Browsing window	Displays the webpage content for the site you are visiting.
Home button	Displays the website you have set as your home page.
View favorites button	Displays a list of websites you have saved as favorites.
Tools button	Displays a menu from which you can access options for printing, security, zoom setting, and managing add-ons.

2 At the top of your screen, click in the **address bar** to select the current URL, type **usa.gov** and then press Enter.

Microsoft also refers to the address bar as the *One Box*, because it serves as both an address and search bar. In this textbook, the term *address bar* will be used to refer to the One Box.

If you completed Project 1A on the same computer, the autocomplete feature may fill in URLs for you, because the app version of Internet Explorer 10 that you used from the Start screen shares information and settings with the desktop version.

The address bar, based on the first few characters that you type, will search across your history and favorites displaying matches. When you see a match, click it to avoid retyping the entire URL of a site you have visited previously.

3 Click in the **address bar** to select the URL text, type **whitehouse.gov** and then press Enter.

Unless you open a new tab, a new URL opens its website on the first tab.

4 To the immediate right of the **Page tab** for **The White House**, point to the new tab to display the **New Tab** button , and then click one time to open a new tab. Compare your screen with Figure 1.25.

A new tab opens; The White House website remains open on the previous tab. Tiles for sites that you visit frequently or visited recently display so that you can go to them quickly if you want to do so when you open a new tab.

More Knowledge   **To Set Your Home Page**

You can set one or more sites to open as your home page. To do so, display the site or group of sites that you want to set as your home page or home page group. Then point to a blank area above or to the right of the Address bar, right-click, and if necessary, display the Command bar. On the Command bar, click the Home button arrow , click Add or change home page, and then select the appropriate option button. You can also click the Home button arrow to remove one or more sites from your Home group.

FIGURE 1.25

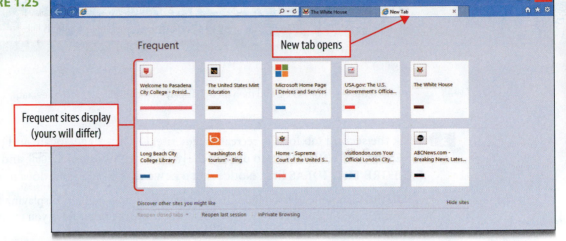

ANOTHER WAY   Press Ctrl + T to open a new tab.

5 With the insertion point blinking in the **address bar**, type **recreation.gov** and then press Enter to display the website for **Recreation.gov**.

6 Open new tabs for the following sites, and then compare your screen with Figure 1.26:

www.cr.nps.gov

www.usbg.gov

www.cfa.gov

FIGURE 1.26

"Welcome to the Commission of Fine Arts", from www.CFA.gov.

7 At the bottom of your screen, on the taskbar, *point* to the **Internet Explorer** icon [e] to display a thumbnail for each open tab. Compare your screen with Figure 1.27, and then leave these tabs open for the next activity.

Here you can see the websites that you have open in Internet Explorer, and you can navigate to a site by clicking its thumbnail image.

FIGURE 1.27

Five thumbnails display

Internet Explorer icon
on the taskbar

"Welcome to the Commission of Fine Arts", from www.CFA.gov.

Activity 1.07 | Opening Links with Internet Explorer 10 in the Desktop

1 Click the next to last tab, for the United States Botanic Garden, to display it in the **browsing window**. Locate the group of links for **ABOUT US**, **GARDENS**, **VISIT** and so on, and then point to **GARDENS** to display the [🖑] pointer.

2 Press Ctrl + Shift, and then click the **GARDENS** link to open this webpage in a new tab. Compare your screen with Figure 1.28.

FIGURE 1.28

New tab displays website for GARDENS link

"United States Botanic Garden", from usbg.gov/gardens

 ANOTHER WAY   Point to the link, right-click, and then on the displayed menu, click Open in new tab.

3 Click the second tab for the **recreation.gov** site. On this page, locate and point to the link for **EXPLORE TRIP IDEAS** to display the 🖐 pointer, hold down Ctrl, and then click the **EXPLORE TRIP IDEAS** link. Notice that a new tab is created but does not open.

Use this technique to open links in separate tabs without actually displaying them. When you are finished viewing the active page, you can investigate the other links you opened. Additionally, the tabs are colored to match so that you know they are related.

4 Click the tab for **The White House**, and then notice that the two tabs from the **recreation.gov** site are the same color. Compare your screen with Figure 1.29.

When you open a link from a webpage, Internet Explorer 10 automatically includes them in a color-coded group.

FIGURE 1.29

New tab site for EXPLORE TRIP IDEAS link

Tabs in same color

whitehouse.gov

5 Point to either of shaded tabs for the **recreation.gov** site, and then right-click to display a menu. Compare your screen with Figure 1.30.

When tabs are in a group, you can use various commands to close the group or ungroup a tab from its group.

FIGURE 1.30

Commands that can be applied to tabs

whitehouse.gov

6 At the bottom of the displayed menu, click **Show tabs on a separate row**, and then compare your screen with Figure 1.31.

Some computer users prefer to show the address bar above the tabs row in this manner. If you typically have many tabs open, you might prefer this arrangement.

FIGURE 1.31

Tabs display on a separate row

whitehouse.gov

7 To capture a screenshot, hold down 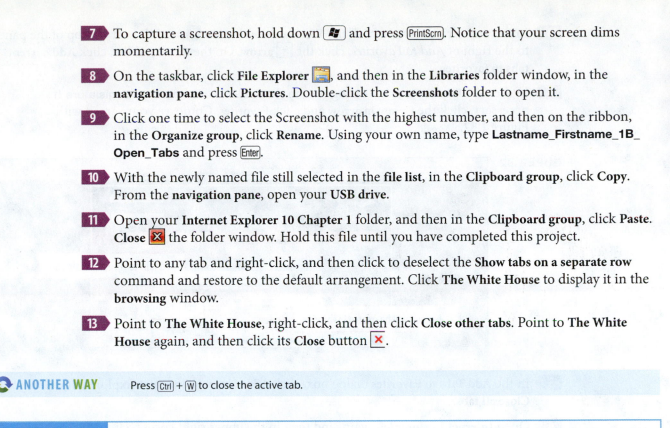 and press (PrintScrn). Notice that your screen dims momentarily.

8 On the taskbar, click **File Explorer** , and then in the **Libraries** folder window, in the **navigation pane**, click **Pictures**. Double-click the **Screenshots** folder to open it.

9 Click one time to select the Screenshot with the highest number, and then on the ribbon, in the **Organize group**, click **Rename**. Using your own name, type **Lastname_Firstname_1B_ Open_Tabs** and press (Enter).

10 With the newly named file still selected in the **file list**, in the **Clipboard group**, click **Copy**. From the **navigation pane**, open your **USB drive**.

11 Open your **Internet Explorer 10 Chapter 1** folder, and then in the **Clipboard group**, click **Paste**. **Close** the folder window. Hold this file until you have completed this project.

12 Point to any tab and right-click, and then click to deselect the **Show tabs on a separate row** command and restore to the default arrangement. Click **The White House** to display it in the **browsing** window.

13 Point to **The White House**, right-click, and then click **Close other tabs**. Point to **The White House** again, and then click its **Close** button .

🔁 **ANOTHER WAY**   Press (Ctrl) + (W) to close the active tab.

More Knowledge   **Cycling Through Open Tabs**

Hold down (Ctrl) and press (Tab) to cycle through and display all open tabs.

Objective 7   Organize Favorites and Manage Browsing History

The *Favorites Center* is a list of links to websites that is saved in your web browser. Saving a website as a favorite allows you to return to it quickly. For example, if you have a favorite health site that you visit frequently, you can save that site's address as a Favorite. Returning to the site requires only one or two clicks instead of typing a complete URL.

You can create a folder to organize your favorite links into groups that are meaningful to you. Then, you can either open one site from the folder, or open all the sites in the folder with a single click.

Activity 1.08 │ Organizing Favorites and Creating a Favorites Folder

In this activity, you will help Barbara and Steven organize a number of sites that they believe will be useful to those who are conducting research for the new hotel in Washington, D.C.

1 **Close** any open windows. On the taskbar, click **Internet Explorer** , click in the **address bar**, type **house.gov** and then press (Enter).

2 Click the **New Tab** button , type **senate.gov** and then press (Enter).

Barbara and Steven know that one thing managers will be looking for is information about the popular locations that both tourists and business visitors will want to know about when they are guests at the hotel.

3 In the upper right corner, click the **View favorites** button ⭐, and then at the top of the pane, to the right of *Add to Favorites*, click the ⏷ **arrow**. On the displayed list, click **Add current tabs to favorites**.

4 In the **Add Tabs to Favorites** dialog box, in the **Folder Name** box, type **Legislature** If necessary, click the **Create in arrow** and click **Favorites**. Compare your screen with Figure 1.32.

FIGURE 1.32

5 In the **Add Tabs to Favorites** dialog box, click **Add**. **Close** ❌ Internet Explorer, and then click **Close all tabs**.

6 Open **Internet Explorer** 🅴 again, and then in the upper right corner, click the **View favorites** button ⭐. If necessary, at the top of the displayed list, click the **Favorites tab**. Click **Legislature** to expand the list, and then point to the arrow to the right of Legislature to display the ScreenTip. Compare your screen with Figure 1.33.

FIGURE 1.33

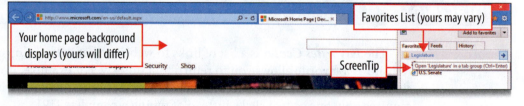

7 To the right of Legislature, click the **arrow** to open the entire group; notice that because they are in a group, the tabs are colored to match. Point to the tab for your home page, right-click, and then click **Close tab** so that only the two **Legislature tabs** display.

From the Favorites List, you can also click one of the links individually to open just one of the links.

8 Display the tab for the **U.S. Senate**, locate and point to the link for **VISITORS** to display the 👆 pointer, and then click the link. Then locate and click the link for **Planning Your Trip**. If these links are not available, click another suitable link.

9 Click the **View favorites** button ⭐, click **Add to favorites**, and then in the **Add a Favorite** dialog box, click the **Create in arrow**. Compare your screen with Figure 1.34.

FIGURE 1.34

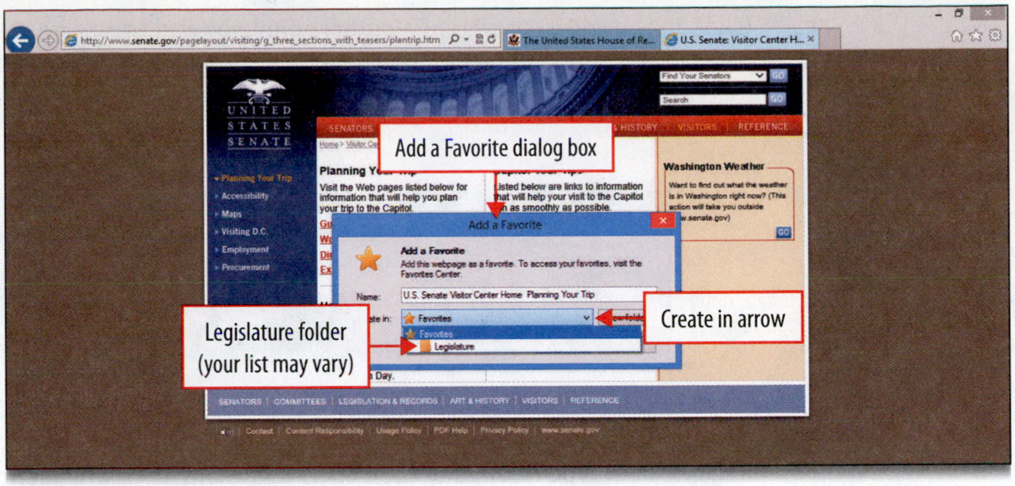

www.senate.gov

10 ▶ On the displayed list, click the **Legislature** folder, and then click the **Add** button.

The link is added to the folder *Legislature*.

11 ▶ **Close** ☒ Internet Explorer, and then click **Close all tabs**.

Activity 1.09 │ Using the Favorites Bar

You can display a **Favorites bar**, which is a toolbar that displays directly below the address bar and to which you can add or drag web addresses you use frequently.

1 ▶ On the taskbar, click **Internet Explorer** 🅴. Point to an empty area above or to the right of the **address bar**, right-click, and then compare your screen with Figure 1.35.

FIGURE 1.35

2 ▶ On the menu, click **Favorites bar**, and then notice the **Favorites bar** under your **address ba**r.

3 ▶ Click in the **address bar** to select the existing URL, type **weather.gov** and then press Enter.

4 ▶ Directly below the **address bar**, click the **Add to Favorites bar** ⭐ button. Compare your screen with Figure 1.36.

FIGURE 1.36

National Weather Service

5 Click in the **address bar**, type **visitthecapitol.gov** and press Enter. At the left end of the **address bar**, point to the **Capitol building logo**, hold down the left mouse button, and then drag the logo onto the **Favorites bar** until a black line displays to the right of the NOAA's site, as shown in Figure 1.37.

FIGURE 1.37

visitthecapitol.gov

6 On the **Favorites bar**, point to the **NOAA's** site, right-click, and then click **Rename**. In the **Rename** box, type **NOAA** and then click **OK**. Using the same technique, rename *Welcome to the U.S. Capitol* link **US Capitol** Compare your screen with Figure 1.38.

You can change and shorten the names on your Favorites bar to make additional space. When you have more Favorites than the bar can accommodate, double chevrons will display at the right, which when clicked will display a continuation of the list.

FIGURE 1.38

visitthecapitol.gov

7 Click in the **address bar**, type **www.archives.gov** and press Enter, and then drag its logo to the **Favorites bar** to the right of **US Capitol**.

8 To capture a screenshot, hold down [⊞] and press PrintScrn. Notice that your screen dims momentarily.

9 On the taskbar, click **File Explorer** 📁, and then in the **Libraries** folder window, in the **navigation pane**, click **Pictures**. Double-click the **Screenshots** folder to open it.

10 Click one time to select the Screenshot with the highest number, and then on the ribbon, in the **Organize group**, click **Rename**. Using your own name, type **Lastname_Firstname_1B_Favorites** and press Enter.

11 With the newly named file still selected in the **file list**, in the **Clipboard group**, click **Copy**. From the **navigation pane**, open your **USB drive**.

12 Open your **Internet Explorer 10 Chapter 1** folder, and then in the **Clipboard group**, click **Paste**. **Close** ✖ the folder window. Hold this file until you have completed this project.

13 Point to the **National Archives** link on the **Favorites bar**, right-click, and then click **Delete**. By using the same technique, delete the links for the **US Capitol** and **NOAA**.

14 **Close** ✖ Internet Explorer.

On your own computer, if you want to do so, display the Favorites bar and place links to the sites you use most frequently on it. For other favorites sites, add them to the Favorites Center.

Activity 1.10 | Viewing and Deleting Browsing History

Recall that as you browse the web, Internet Explorer stores information about the websites you visit. This is referred to as your browsing history. You can view and delete your browsing history while using the desktop version of Internet Explorer 10.

1 On the taskbar, click **Internet Explorer** . Click the **View favorites** button , and then at the top of the pane click the **History tab**. Under **History**, click the **arrow**, and then if necessary, click **View By Date**. If necessary, click **Today**. Display the list again, click **View By Order Visited Today**, and then compare your screen with Figure 1.39.

Here you can view a list of the sites you visited today.

FIGURE 1.39

2 To the right or above the **address bar**, right-click, and then click **Command bar** to display this toolbar. Click **Safety**.

Here you can select InPrivate Browsing in the same manner you practiced using Internet Explorer from the Start screen.

3 Click **Delete browsing history**.

Here you can delete all of your web browsing history, or individually select one or more categories of files to delete.

4 Unless you are working on your own computer and you do not want to delete any files, click the **Delete** button, and then wait a few moments for the deletion to complete.

Deleting all browsing history does not delete your list of Favorites. This action deletes only temporary files, your browsing history, cookies, and saved form information passwords—if their checkboxes are selected.

If you perform this action on your own computer, it might take a few seconds longer to display sites again the first time you access them. After that, the system will rebuild your browsing history as you browse the web.

5 **Close** Internet Explorer.

More Knowledge | **Close Internet Explorer after Deleting Browsing History**

Close Internet Explorer after deleting your browsing history to clear cookies that are still in memory from your current browsing session. This is especially important when using a public computer such as in your college computer lab.

Objective 8 | Print, Zoom, and Change the Text Size of Webpages

By default, Internet Explorer 10 will shrink a webpage's text just enough to ensure that the entire page prints properly. The Page Zoom feature enables you to increase or decrease the page size for easier viewing. You can also adjust the size of displayed text.

Activity 1.11 | Printing Webpages

Internet Explorer 10 provides useful options for formatting and then printing a webpage. In the following activity, you will work with Barbara and Steven to print a webpage.

1 **Close** ⊠ any open windows. On the taskbar, click **Internet Explorer** 🅴, click in the **address bar**, type **usa.gov** and then press `Enter`. Then click the link for **Government Agencies**.

The site usa.gov serves as the official *portal* for the United States government displays. A portal is a website that displays news, content, and links that are of interest to a specific audience; for example, individuals who need information about government agencies and services.

2 On the **Command bar**, locate and click the **Print button arrow** 🖶 to display a menu. Compare your screen with Figure 1.40.

FIGURE 1.40

3 On the menu, click **Print Preview**. Compare your screen with Figure 1.41, and then take a moment to study the parts of the Print Preview window described in the table in Figure 1.42.

Recall that Internet Explorer will shrink the page as necessary to fit horizontally on the selected paper size. You can also drag the margins by using the adjust margin buttons on this Print Preview screen.

FIGURE 1.41

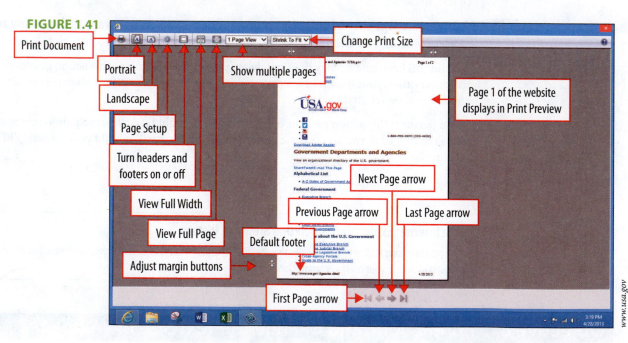

PARTS OF THE PRINT PREVIEW WINDOW IN INTERNET EXPLORER 10	
Parts	**Description**
Adjust margin buttons	Adjusts the left, right, top, and bottom margins by dragging.
Change Print Size	Stretches or shrinks the page size to fill the printed page.
First Page arrow	Displays the first page of a multiple page preview screen.
Landscape	Prints the page in landscape orientation, in which the paper is wider than it is tall.
Last Page arrow	Displays the last page of a multiple page preview screen.
Next Page arrow	Displays the next page of a multiple page preview screen.
Page indicator	Indicates the page displayed and the total number of pages.
Page Setup	Opens the Page Setup dialog box, in which you can change paper size, orientation, margins, and header and footer options.
Portrait	Prints the page in portrait orientation, in which the paper is taller than it is wide.
Previous Page arrow	Displays the previous page of a multiple page preview screen.
Print Document	Opens the Print dialog box, enabling you to print the page using the current settings.
Show multiple pages	Displays multiple pages on the preview screen.
Turn headers or footers on or off	Turns the display of headers and footers off or on in the manner of a toggle button.
View Full Page	Zooms the webpage to show the full webpage in the preview screen.
View Full Width	Zooms the webpage to the width of the preview screen.

FIGURE 1.42

4 On the **Print Preview Command bar**, click the **Show multiple pages arrow** ☑, and then click **2 Page View**.

> At 100%, this webpage, as currently formatted, will print on two pages; your system may automatically adjust.

5 On the **Command bar**, to the right of *Shrink To Fit*, click the **Change Print Size button arrow** ☑, and then from the displayed list, click **Custom**. In the % box, type **85** and press Enter. Compare your screen with Figure 1.43.

FIGURE 1.43

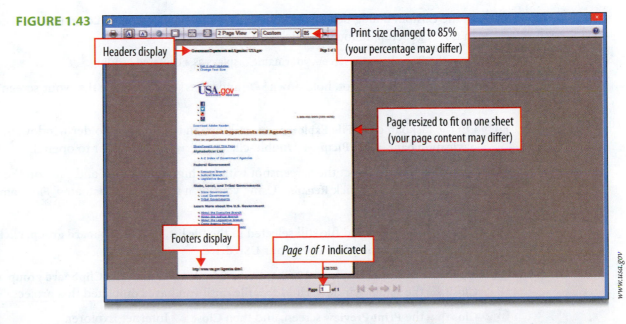

Print size changed to 85% (your percentage may differ)

Headers display

Page resized to fit on one sheet (your page content may differ)

Footers display

Page 1 of 1 indicated

🔄 **ANOTHER WAY**   Experiment with percentages on the list, or by typing in the Custom box, to shrink the page to print the way you want it to—on one or more pages.

6 On the **Command bar**, to the right of *2 Page View*, click the **Show multiple pages button arrow** ☑, and then click **1 Page View** to return to that view and center the page on the Preview screen.

7 On the **Command bar**, click the **Page Setup** button ⚙. Compare your screen with Figure 1.44.

Here you can change or add to the headers and footers on a printed webpage.

By default there are two headers, one left aligned and one right aligned, which will display the page title and the Page # of total pages. Similarly, there are two footers, one left aligned and one right aligned, which will display the URL and the date in short format.

The default setting for the centered header and footer is *Empty*. You can change any of the headers and footers by clicking the arrow and selecting an item or by selecting Custom and creating a new entry. You can also change the font of the headers and footers.

FIGURE 1.44

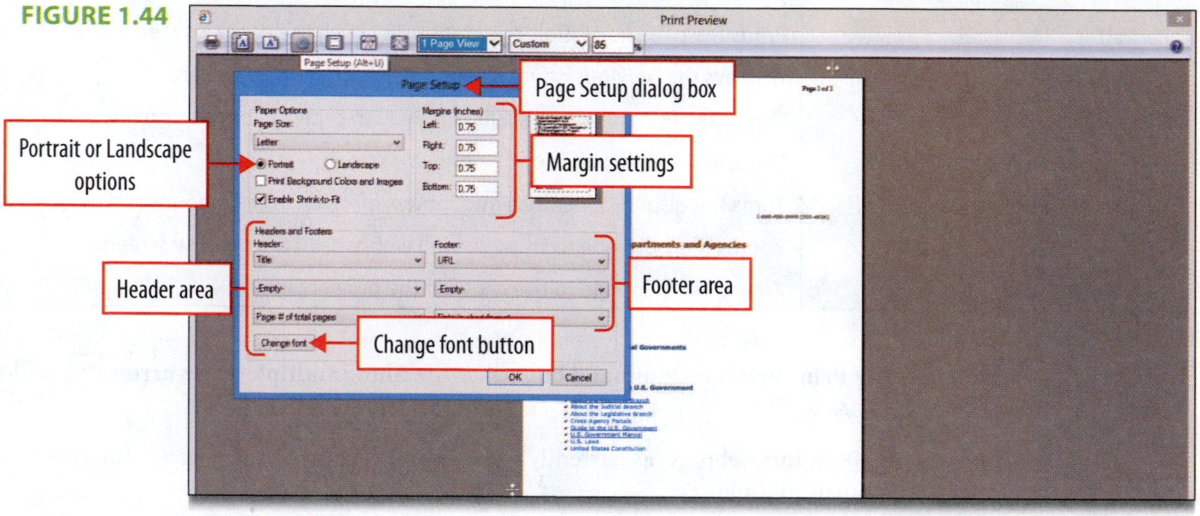

8 Under **Footer**, click the second arrow, and then click **Custom**.

Here you can enter a centered footer.

9 In the **Custom** dialog box, using your own name, type **Firstname Lastname** and then click **OK**. In the **Page Setup** dialog box, click **OK**.

In the Print Preview screen, your name displays as a centered heading.

10 To capture a screenshot, hold down ⊞ and press PrintScrn. Notice that your screen dims momentarily.

11 On the taskbar, click **File Explorer** 📁, and then in the **Libraries** folder window, in the **navigation pane**, click **Pictures**. Double-click the **Screenshots** folder to open it.

12 Click one time to select the Screenshot with the highest number, and then on the ribbon, in the **Organize group**, click **Rename**. Using your own name, type **Lastname_Firstname_1B_Print** and press Enter.

13 With the newly named file still selected in the **file list**, in the **Clipboard group**, click **Copy**. From the **navigation pane**, open your **USB drive**.

14 Open your **Internet Explorer 10 Chapter 1** folder, and then in the **Clipboard group**, click **Paste**. **Close** ❎ the folder window. Hold this file until you have completed this project.

15 **Close** ❎ the **Print Preview** screen, and then **Close** ❎ Internet Explorer.

Activity 1.12 | Zooming and Changing the Text Size of Webpages

1 ▶ **Close** ☒ any open windows. On the taskbar, click **Internet Explorer** , click in the **address bar**, type **senate.gov** and press Enter. On the **Command bar**, click the **Page** button, point to **Zoom**, and then click **200%**.

> The view of the page is increased to 200%. Increasing the Zoom level increases the size of everything on the page, including graphics and controls.

2 ▶ Using the technique you just practiced, change the **Zoom** level to **50%**.

3 ▶ Hold down Ctrl and then turn your mouse wheel backward and forward to increase and decrease the zoom.

> This is a useful technique if you want to briefly magnify some text that is difficult to read or to examine a photo closely.

4 ▶ Change the **Zoom** level back to **100%**.

5 ▶ Open a **New Tab** , type **www.archives.gov** and then press Enter. On the **Command bar**, click the **Page** button, and then point to **Text size**.

> The default text size is Medium, but if you would like to see more text on the screen you can set a smaller text size. If you have difficulty reading webpages on your screen, you can set a larger text size.
>
> Changing the text size affects only the text—graphics and controls continue to display in their original size.

6 ▶ On the displayed submenu, click **Largest**, and notice that the text on your screen is enlarged. Compare your screen with Figure 1.45.

FIGURE 1.45

archives.gov

7 ▶ Using the technique you just practiced, return the **Text Size** to **Medium**.

8 ▶ **Close** ☒ Internet Explorer.

> **N O T E** | **The Text Size of Some Webpages Is Set by the Person Who Created the Page**
>
> The creator of the webpage may set a specific text size that you cannot change with the Text Size command. If you want to do so, you can override as follows: click the Tools button on the Command bar, click Internet Options, on the General tab, click the Accessibility button, and then select the Ignore font sizes specified on webpages check box.

Objective 9   Save Webpage Information

You can save an entire webpage, an image on a webpage, or selected text from a webpage. Doing so is a good way to capture information to which you want to refer to later without accessing the Internet.

Activity 1.13 │ Saving Webpage Information

1 ▸ **Close** ⊠ any open windows. On the taskbar, click **Internet Explorer** 🅮, click in the **address bar**, type **nga.gov** and then press Enter.

2 ▸ On the **Command bar**, click the **Page** button, and then click **Save as**. At the bottom of the displayed **Save Webpage** dialog box, click the **Save as type arrow**, and then compare your screen with Figure 1.46.

To save all files associated with the page, including graphics, frames, and style sheets in their original format, you can use the file format *Webpage, complete (*.htm;*.html)*.

To save all information as a single file, you can use the file format *Web Archive, single file (*.mht)*.

To save just the current HTML page, without graphics, sounds, or other files, you can use the file format *Webpage, HTML only (*.htm;*.html)*. To save just the text from the current webpage, you can use the file format *Text File (*.txt)*.

FIGURE 1.46

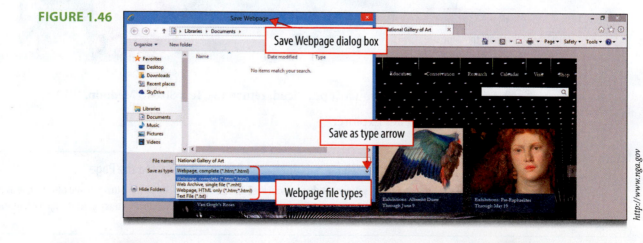

3 ▸ **Close** ⊠ the **Save Webpage** dialog box without saving, and then **Close** ⊠ Internet Explorer.

Objective 10 | Protect Your Data

Windows 8 and Internet Explorer 10 provide a variety of ways to protect your personal data and your electronic transactions.

Activity 1.14 | Using the Internet Explorer 10 Pop-up Blocker and Information Bar

A *pop-up* is a small web browser window that displays on top of the website you are viewing; pop-ups are usually created by advertisers. *Pop-up Blocker* is a feature in Internet Explorer that enables you to limit or block most pop-ups. The Notification bar displays information about downloads, blocked pop-up windows, and other activities. Pop-up Blocker is enabled by default. To turn it off or change the settings, display the Tools menu as shown in Figure 1.47.

FIGURE 1.47

By displaying the Pop-up Blocker Settings dialog box, you can *allow* pop-ups from specific websites as shown in Figure 1.48. You can also select the Blocking level and decide whether to play a sound or show the Notification bar when a pop-up is blocked. These default settings are appropriate for most computer users. Some sites request that you allow pop-ups from their site, and if you trust the site, it is safe to do so.

Because the Notification bar displays on a site when a pop-up is blocked, you always have the choice of viewing the pop-up message if you want to do so. Click the Notification bar and then click Show Blocked Pop-up. From the Notification bar, you can also click to temporarily accept pop-ups from a specific site.

FIGURE 1.48

The Notification bar will display if:

- A site tries to install an ActiveX control, install an updated ActiveX control, install an add-on program, run an ActiveX control in an unsafe manner, or run active content.
- A site tries to download a file to your computer.
- Your security settings are below the recommended levels.
- You started Internet Explorer with add-ons disabled.

One advantage of the Notification bar is that you are not required to attend to it. For example, if you display a site by mistakenly typing an incorrect URL, you can ignore the Notification bar. If you want to proceed with using a feature of the displayed site, click the message and then take appropriate action.

To check how well you can identify pop-up blocking functions, take a moment to answer the following questions:

1 By default, Pop-up Blocker is _____.

2 You always have the choice of _____ a pop-up message if you want to do so.

3 One common reason that the Notification bar will display is if a website tries to install, update, or run in an unsafe manner any type of _____ control.

4 The Notification bar commonly displays if a site tries to _____ a file to your computer.

5 One advantage of the Notification bar is that you are not _____ to do anything with it.

Activity 1.15 | Protecting against Malware

Internet Explorer will warn you when webpages try to install software by displaying the Notification bar. There are additional ways in which Internet Explorer provides safety features to protect your computer against malware.

Internet Explorer's **protected mode** makes it more difficult for malicious software to be installed on your computer by preventing a downloaded program from making any direct changes to the system. It also allows you to install *wanted* ActiveX controls or add-ons when you are logged on as an administrator. Protected mode is on by default and you will see it indicated in the status bar. One way that protected mode helps protect your computer from malicious downloads is by restricting where files can be saved without your consent.

Windows Defender is a spyware scanning and removal tool included with Windows 8. By default, Windows Defender, when enabled, scans your computer for spyware automatically daily. During the scan, Windows Defender takes automatic action on various items, depending on your preferences. If any spyware is found, you are prompted with options to deal with each threat by selecting Ignore, Quarantine, Remove, or Always Allow. Windows Defender constantly updates its definitions so that it can find new spyware threats that emerge on the Internet.

The first step in using Windows Defender is to make sure it is enabled on your computer. To do so, open the Control Panel, type defender in the Search box, and then click Windows Defender. To enable or change the settings of Windows Defender, click the Settings tab as shown in Figure 1.49.

FIGURE 1.49

A *certificate* is a digital document that verifies the identity of a person or indicates the security of a website. Certificates are issued by trusted companies known as **Certification Authorities**. Certificates make secure transactions on the Internet possible. When you visit a secure website in Internet Explorer, a padlock icon will display in the address bar indicating that a digital certificate identifies the site. As shown in Figure 1.50, you can click the padlock icon to display information about the certificate.

FIGURE 1.50

You can see specific information about the issuer of the certificate by clicking *View certificates*. You will commonly see such certificate information on any site where financial transactions are involved.

Phishing is a technique used to trick computer users into revealing personal or financial information through an email message or a website. The message or site appears to come from a trusted source but actually directs recipients to provide information to a fraudulent website.

SmartScreen Filter is a feature in Internet Explorer that helps detect phishing websites and websites that distribute malware. SmartScreen Filter runs in the background and protects you by comparing the addresses of websites you visit against a list of sites reported to Microsoft as legitimate. This list is stored on your computer. It also analyzes the sites you visit to see if they have characteristics common to a phishing site.

To manually check a website that you find suspicious, navigate to the site you want to check, on the Command bar, click Safety, point to SmartScreen Filter, click Check this website, and then click OK. If a website is flagged as suspicious, you should not submit any personal or financial information to it unless you are certain that the site is trustworthy. Suspicious sites are flagged by Internet Explorer by displaying the address bar in yellow along with a message. For more information about how Internet Explorer handles phishing, in the Windows Help and Support window, search for phishing and click SmartScreen Filter: frequently asked questions.

Another feature in Internet Explorer 10 is *Do Not Track*, which sends a signal to websites that you prefer not to have information about your visit used in a manner to track you as you browse the web.

To check how well you understand data and family protection, take a moment to answer the following questions:

1. A certificate can verify the _____ of a website.

2. Certificates make _____ transactions on the web possible.

3. When you visit a secure website, the address bar displays a _____ icon.

4. A technique to trick computer users into revealing personal information is _____.

5. If the SmartScreen Filter in Internet Explorer suspects a website of having phishing characteristics, it will display a message and display the address bar in _____.

END | You have completed Project 1B

END OF CHAPTER

SUMMARY

Browsing the web using Internet Explorer 10 from the Start screen displays a full-screen immersive view of websites without distraction. This version of Internet Explorer 10 is useful for touch devices like tablets.

A search provider—or search engine—provides search capabilities on the web. The default search provider in Internet Explorer 10 is Microsoft's Bing, and you can also install the Google app to search with Google.

Internet Explorer stores information about websites you visit. Use InPrivate Browsing to browse without any information being stored. By opening an InPrivate tab, information is deleted when you close the tab.

IE 10 has two versions—the Start screen app version and the desktop app version. Use whichever version is convenient and comfortable for you. Both programs share the same information and underlying technology.

GO! LEARN IT ONLINE

Review the concepts and key terms in this chapter by completing these online challenges, which you can find at **www.pearsonhighered.com/go**.

Matching and Multiple Choice:
Answer matching and multiple choice questions to test what you learned in this chapter. MyITLab°

END OF CHAPTER

REVIEW AND ASSESSMENT GUIDE FOR INTERNET EXPLORER 10 CHAPTER 1

Your instructor may assign one or more of these projects to help you review the chapter and assess your mastery and understanding of the chapter.

Review and Assessment Guide for Internet Explorer 10 Chapter 1			
Project	**Apply Skills from These Chapter Objectives**	**Project Type**	**Project Location**
1C	Objectives 1–5 from Project 1A	**1C Skills Review** A guided review of the skills from Project 1A.	On the following pages
1D	Objectives 6–10 from Project 1B	**1D Skills Review** A guided review of the skills from Project 1B.	On the following pages
1E	Objectives 1–5 from Project 1A	**1E Mastery** A demonstration of your mastery of the skills in Project 1A with decision making.	On the following pages
1F	Objectives 6–10 from Project 1B	**1F Mastery** A demonstration of your mastery of the skills in Project 1B with decision making.	On the following pages
1G	Combination of Objectives from Projects 1A and 1B	**1G GO! Think** A demonstration of your understanding of the chapter concepts applied in a manner that you would outside of college. An analytic rubric helps you and your instructor grade the quality of your work by comparing it to the work an expert in the discipline would create.	On the following pages
1H	Combination of Objectives from Projects 1A and 1B	**1H GO! Think** A demonstration of your understanding of the chapter concepts applied in a manner that you would outside of college. An analytic rubric helps you and your instructor grade the quality of your work by comparing it to the work an expert in the discipline would create.	On the following pages
1I	Combination of Objectives from Projects 1A and 1B	**1I GO! Think** A demonstration of your understanding of the chapter concepts applied in a manner that you would outside of college. An analytic rubric helps you and your instructor grade the quality of your work by comparing it to the work an expert in the discipline would create.	On the following pages

GLOSSARY

GLOSSARY OF CHAPTER KEY TERMS

Address bar In Internet Explorer 10, the area in which you can type a URL to visit a website; displays at the bottom of the screen in the Start screen version of IE 10 and at the top of the screen in the desktop version of IE 10.

Blog An online journal or column used to publish personal or company information in an informal manner.

Browsing The term used to describe the process of using your computer to view webpages.

Browsing history The information stored by Internet Explorer about the sites you have visited and the information you have typed into a site.

Browsing window In Internet Explorer 10, the area of the screen in which the webpage displays.

Certificate A digital document that verifies the identity of a person or indicates the security of a website.

Certification Authorities Companies, for example VeriSign, that issue digital certificates.

Cookies Small text files that websites put on your computer to store information about you and your preferences, for example logon information.

Country codes Top level domains for countries, for example *.ca* for Canada.

Do Not Track A feature in Internet Explorer 10 that sends a signal to websites that you prefer not to have information about your visit used in a manner to track you as you browse the web.

Domain name An organization's unique name on the Internet, which consists of a chosen name combined with a top level domain such as *.com* or *.org* or *.gov*.

Favorites bar A toolbar in Internet Explorer 10 that you can optionally display directly below the address bar and to which you can add or drag web addresses you use frequently.

Favorites Center A list of links to websites that is saved in your web browser.

Home page On your own computer, the webpage you have selected—or that is set by default—to display on your computer when you start Internet Explorer; when visiting a website, the starting point for the remainder of the pages on that site.

http The protocol prefix for HyperText Transfer Protocol.

HyperText Transfer Protocol The set of communication rules used by your computer to connect to servers on the web.

IE 10 The acronym for Internet Explorer 10.

InPrivate Browsing A feature in Internet Explorer 10 with which you can browse the web without storing data about your browsing session; useful when using a public computer.

Internet Explorer 10 The web browser software developed by Microsoft Corporation that is included with Windows 8; there are two versions that use the same underlying information and technology—one version for the Start screen and one version for the desktop.

Internet Explorer 10 in the desktop The term for the version of Internet Explorer 10 used on the desktop.

One Box Another name for the address bar in Internet Explorer 10 in the desktop, because it serves as both an address and search bar.

Phishing A technique used to trick computer users into revealing personal or financial information through an email message or a website.

Plug-ins Small programs that add capabilities to the browser software such as playing video or scanning for viruses.

Pop-up A small web browser window that displays on top of the website you are viewing, and which is usually created by advertisers.

Pop-up Blocker A feature in Internet Explorer that enables you to block most pop-ups.

Portal A website that displays news, content, and links that are of interest to a specific audience.

Protected mode A feature in Internet Explorer that makes it more difficult for malicious software to be installed on your computer by preventing a downloaded program from making any direct changes to the system.

Protocol prefix The letters that represent a set of communication rules used by a computer to connect to another computer.

Search engine A computer program that searches for specific words and returns a list of documents in which the search term was found.

Search provider A website that provides search capabilities on the web.

SmartScreen Filter A feature in Internet Explorer that helps detect phishing websites and websites that distribute malware.

Social Results Bing search results that match your search intent with relevant people and experts.

Sponsored links Paid advertisements shown as links, typically for products and services related to your search term.

Surfing The process of navigating the Internet either for a particular item or for anything that is of interest, and quickly moving from one item to another.

Tabbed browsing A feature in Internet Explorer that enables you to open multiple websites and then switch among them.

Tabs bar In the Start screen version of Internet Explorer 10, the bar that displays a tile for each webpage that you currently have open—only one tab displays because only one webpage is open.

Temporary Internet files Copies of webpages, images, and media that you have downloaded from the web, which makes viewing faster the next time you visit a site that you have visited before.

TLD The acronym for top level domain.

Top level domain The ending letters of a URL such as *.com*, *.org*, and so on.

Uniform Resource Locator An address that uniquely identifies a location on the Internet.

URL The acronym for Uniform Resource Locator.

Web browser A software program with which you display webpages and navigate the Internet.

Web log The term from which *blog* is derived; an online journal or column used to publish personal or company information in an informal manner.

Windows Defender A spyware scanning and removal tool included with Windows 8.

CHAPTER REVIEW

Apply 1A skills from these Objectives:

1 Navigate with Internet Explorer 10
2 Navigate with Tabs
3 Search the Internet
4 Browse with InPrivate
5 Configure Internet Explorer 10

Skills Review | Project 1C Navigate Internet Explorer 10

PROJECT FILES

For Project 1C, you will need the following files:

Your USB flash drive containing the student data files
ie01_1C_Answer_Sheet (Word document)

You will save your file as:

Lastname_Firstname_1C_Answer_Sheet

1 ▶ Display the **Start screen**; point to the upper left corner, and then **Close** any open apps. Display the **desktop**. **Close** ⊠ any open desktop windows. On the taskbar, click **File Explorer**. In the **navigation pane**, click your **USB drive** that contains the student files for this textbook, and then navigate to **Chapter_Files** ▶ **Chapter_01**. Double-click the Word file **ie01_1C_Answer_Sheet** to open Word and display the document. If necessary, at the top, click **Enable editing**; be sure the window is maximized. In the upper left corner, click **FILE**, click **Save As**, click **Computer**, and then click **Browse** to display the **Save As** dialog box. In the **navigation pane**, click your **USB drive** and then double-click to open your **Internet Explorer 10 Chapter 1** folder. Using your own name, **Save** the document as **Lastname_Firstname_1C_Answer_Sheet** Click **Save**.

On the taskbar, click the **Word** button to minimize the window and leave your Word document accessible from the taskbar. **Close** the **Chapter_01** folder window. As you complete each step in this project, write the letter of your answer on a piece of paper; you will fill in your Answer Sheet after you complete all the steps in this project.

Display the **Start screen**, and then click the **Internet Explorer** tile. In the **address bar**, click the existing URL to select it, type **microsoft.com** and then press Enter. Which of the following is *not* true?

A. From this screen, you can pin this site to your Start screen.

B. From this screen, you can go back to the previous webpage that was displayed.

C. From this screen, you can go forward to the next webpage of content.

2 ▶ In the **address bar**, click the existing URL, type **usa.gov** and then press Enter. What is the term used to describe the area in which the information about the government displays?

A. web window

B. browsing window

C. app window

3 ▶ In the **address bar**, which of the following identifies this site's top level domain?

A. .gov

B. usa

C. http

4 ▶ Click the URL in the **address bar**, type **weather.gov** and then press Enter. In the **browsing window**, point to the left center edge of the screen, and then click ◀. What is your result?

A. The webpage for bing.com displays.

B. The webpage for microsoft.com displays.

C. The webpage for usa.gov displays.

(Project 1C Navigate Internet Explorer 10 continues on the next page)

CHAPTER REVIEW

5 Point to an empty area of the **browsing** window to display the ⬉ pointer, and then right-click. What is your result?

A. The address bar displays at the bottom of the screen.

B. The Tabs bar displays at the top of the screen.

C. Both A. and B.

6 In the **Tabs bar**, click the **New Tab** button ⊕. Which of the following is *not* true?

A. The browsing window is empty.

B. A message displays prompting you to type a URL.

C. The insertion point is blinking in the address bar at the bottom of the screen.

7 In the **address bar**, type **nyc.gov/visitors** and press Enter. When the webpage displays, press Ctrl + T to open a new tab, and then type **radiocity.com** and press Enter. Press Ctrl + T to open a new tab, and then type **iloveny.com** and press Enter. Point to an empty area of the **browsing** window to display the ⬉ pointer, and then right-click. Which of the following is true?

A. Five tabs display in the Tabs bar.

B. Four tabs display in the Tabs bar.

C. Three tabs display in the Tabs bar.

8 In the **Tabs bar**, click the tab for **Radio City Music Hall**. Locate the link **GET TICKETS**, point to the link to display the 👆 pointer, right-click, and then click **Open link in new tab**. Point to an empty area of the **browsing window** to display the ⬉ pointer, and then right-click. Which of the following is true?

A. A tab for a Calendar of Events for Radio City Music Hall displays in the Tabs bar.

B. The webpage for I Love NY displays in the browsing window.

C. The usa.gov tab is the active tab.

9 On the **Tabs bar**, click the **Tab tools** button ⊙, and then click **New InPrivate tab**. Which of the following is *not* true?

A. A blue icon labeled *InPrivate* displays in the address bar.

B. The box to type a URL is empty.

C. The Microsoft.com site displays in the browsing window.

10 As the URL, type **amazon.com** and press Enter. Which of the following is *not* true?

A. Anyone who uses your computer will not be able to see that you visited the amazon.com website.

B. Any cookies created by visiting amazon.com will be deleted when you close Internet Explorer.

C. You will not be able to make a purchase at amazon.com because you initiated InPrivate browsing.

To complete this project: Point to the top edge of the screen to display the 👆 pointer, and then drag to the bottom of the screen to close **Internet Explorer**. Click the **Desktop** tile. On the taskbar, click the **Word** button, and then type your answers into the correct boxes. **Save** and **close** your Word document, and submit as directed by your instructor. **Close** all open windows.

END | You have completed Project 1C

CHAPTER REVIEW

Skills Review | Project 1D Using Internet Explorer 10 in the Desktop

PROJECT FILES

For Project 1D, you will need the following files:

Your USB flash drive containing the student data files
ie01_1D_Answer_Sheet (Word document)

You will save your file as:

Lastname_Firstname_1D_Answer_Sheet

1 ▶ Display the **Start screen**; point to the upper left corner, and then **Close** any open apps. Display the **desktop**. **Close** ☒ any open desktop windows. On the taskbar, click **File Explorer**. In the **navigation pane**, click your **USB drive** that contains the student files for this textbook, and then navigate to **Chapter_Files ▶ Chapter_01**. Double-click the Word file **ie01_1D_Answer_Sheet** to open Word and display the document. If necessary, at the top, click **Enable editing**; be sure the window is maximized. In the upper left corner, click **FILE**, click **Save As**, click **Computer**, and then click **Browse** to display the **Save As** dialog box. In the **navigation pane**, click your **USB drive** and then double-click to open your **Internet Explorer 10 Chapter 1** folder. Using your own name, **Save** the document as **Lastname_Firstname_1D_Answer_Sheet** Click **Save**.

On the taskbar, click the **Word** button to minimize the window and leave your Word document accessible from the taskbar. **Close** the **Chapter_01** folder window. As you complete each step in this project, write the letter of your answer on a piece of paper; you will fill in your Answer Sheet after you complete all the steps in this project.

From the taskbar on the desktop, click Internet Explorer. Be sure that you have displayed the **Favorites bar** and the **Command bar**. Click in the **address bar** and navigate to **doh.state.fl.us** Open a New Tab, and then go to the site **miamigov.com** Which of the following is true?

A. The tabs display in alphabetical order by website name.

B. Thumbnails for each open site display.

C. The tabs display in the order they were opened.

2 ▶ On the taskbar, point to the **Internet Explorer** icon 🖉. What is the result?

A. Thumbnail images for each tab display.

B. All of the sites close.

C. A menu displays to close all tabs.

3 ▶ On a **New Tab**, go to the site **ufl.edu** and then click the **View favorites** button. Click **Add to favorites**. What is your result?

A. The Favorites Center pane displays on the left side of the screen.

B. The Create Favorites Folder dialog box displays.

C. The Add a Favorite dialog box displays.

4 ▶ Click **Cancel**. On the displayed home page for **Florida International University**, point to the link for **Athletics** to display the 🖑 pointer, and then right-click. From the displayed shortcut menu, which of the following actions are possible?

A. You can open the Athletics link in a new tab.

B. You can send the Athletics link to your Documents folder.

C. You can create a tab group.

(Project 1D Using Internet Explorer 10 in the Desktop continues on the next page)

CHAPTER REVIEW

5 Click in a blank area of the screen to close the shortcut menu. Click the **View favorites** button to open the **Favorites** pane. Across the top, which tabs display?

A. Favorites, Tab Groups, Feeds

B. Favorites, Feeds, History

C. Favorites, History, Recent Pages

6 Click the **History tab**, and then click the **arrow**. Which of the following is *not* a viewing arrangement?

A. By Date

B. By Favorites

C. By Most Visited

7 Click in a blank area of the screen to close **Favorites** pane. On the **Command bar**, click the **Safety** button, and then click **Delete Browsing History**. According to this information, cookies consist of:

A. Saved information that you have typed into forms.

B. Files stored on your computer by websites to save preferences.

C. Buttons added to the tab row.

8 **Close** the **Delete Browsing History** dialog box. Click the **Tools** button, and then click **Manage add-ons**. At the bottom of the screen, click **Find more toolbars and extensions**. What is your result?

A. A list of add-ons stored on your computer displays.

B. A list of recently used add-ons displays.

C. The Microsoft site for finding and installing new add-ons displays.

9 **Close** the **Add-ons** site and the **Manage Add-ons** window. Open a **New Tab**, and then at the bottom, click **InPrivate Browsing**. What is your result?

A. The Delete Browsing History dialog box displays.

B. A new window opens in which you can type a URL in the Address box.

C. Both A and B.

10 **Close** the **InPrivate** window and **Close** the new tab. With the **FIU** site displayed, click the **Print button arrow**, and then click **Print preview**. Click the **Page Setup** button to display the **Page Setup** dialog box. From this dialog box, which of the following can be changed?

A. Left and right margins

B. Headers and Footers

C. Both A. and B.

To complete this project: On the taskbar, click the **Word** button, and then type your answers into the correct boxes. **Save** and **Close** your Word document, and submit as directed by your instructor. **Close** ☒ all open windows.

END | You have completed Project 1D

CONTENT-BASED ASSESSMENTS

Apply 1A skills from these Objectives:

1 Navigate with Internet Explorer 10

2 Navigate with Tabs

3 Search the Internet

4 Browse with InPrivate

5 Configure Internet Explorer 10

| Mastering Internet Explorer 10 | Project 1E Navigate with Internet Explorer 10 |

In the following Mastering Internet Explorer 10 project, you will open a group of websites on separate tabs. You will capture and save a screen that will look similar to Figure 1.51.

PROJECT FILES

For Project 1E, you will need the following file:

New Screenshot

You will save your file as:

Lastname_Firstname_1E_Gov_Tabs

PROJECT RESULTS

FIGURE 1.51

(Project 1E Navigate with Internet Explorer 10 continues on the next page)

CONTENT-BASED ASSESSMENTS

1 Display your **Start screen**, and then click the **Internet Explorer** tile. In the **address bar**, click to select the existing text, and then type **bls.gov** and press Enter.

2 Open a tab for each of the following sites:

> **defense.gov**
>
> **state.gov**
>
> **ed.gov**
>
> **nih.gov**

3 Display the **Tabs bar**, and then create a screenshot that displays the **Tabs bar** with each of the five sites displayed, copy the screenshot to your **Internet Explorer 10 Chapter 1** folder, and then rename it as **Lastname_Firstname_1E_Gov_Tabs**

4 Submit this file as directed by your instructor. Point to the top edge of the screen to display the 🖑 pointer, and then drag to the bottom of the screen to close **Internet Explorer**.

END | You have completed Project 1E

CONTENT-BASED ASSESSMENTS

Mastering Internet Explorer 10 | Project 1F Using Internet Explorer 10 in the Desktop

In the following Mastering Internet Explorer 10 project, you will open related sites on separate tabs, and then capture and save a screen that will look similar to Figure 1.52.

PROJECT FILES

For Project 1F, you will need the following file:

New Screenshot

You will save your file as:

Lastname_Firstname_1F_Sites

PROJECT RESULTS

FIGURE 1.52

www.nga.gov

(Project 1F Using Internet Explorer 10 in the Desktop continues on the next page)

CONTENT-BASED ASSESSMENTS

Mastering Internet Explorer 10 | **Project 1F Using Internet Explorer 10 in the Desktop** (continued)

1 From the taskbar on your desktop, open **Internet Explorer** and be sure only the tab for your home page displays. Click in the **address bar**, type **usbg.gov** and press Enter. Hold down Ctrl, and then in the navigation bar in this site, click **SUSTAINABILITY** so that a new tab is created for the link and the two tabs are color coded.

2 On a **New Tab**, go to the site **nga.gov** Hold down Ctrl, and then in the navigation bar of this site, click **The Collection** so that a new tab is created for the link and the two tabs are color coded.

3 Create a screenshot, copy the screenshot to your **Internet Explorer 10 Chapter 1** folder, and then rename it as **Lasname_Firstname_1F_Sites** Submit this file as directed by your instructor.

4 **Close** all open windows and **Close** Internet Explorer.

END | You have completed Project 1F

OUTCOMES-BASED ASSESSMENTS

RUBRIC

The following outcomes-based assessments are *open-ended assessments*. That is, there is no specific correct result; your result will depend on your approach to the information provided. Make *Professional Quality* your goal. Use the following scoring rubric to guide you in *how* to approach the problem, and then to evaluate *how well* your approach solves the problem.

The *criteria*—Software Mastery, Content, Format and Layout, and Process—represent the knowledge and skills you have gained that you can apply to solving the problem. The *levels of performance*—Professional Quality, Approaching Professional Quality, or Needs Quality Improvements—help you and your instructor evaluate your result.

	Your completed project is of Professional Quality if you:	Your completed project is Approaching Professional Quality if you:	Your completed project Needs Quality Improvements if you:
1-Software Mastery	Choose and apply the most appropriate skills, tools, and features and identify efficient methods to solve the problem.	Choose and apply some appropriate skills, tools, and features, but not in the most efficient manner.	Choose inappropriate skills, tools, or features, or are inefficient in solving the problem.
2-Content	Construct a solution that is clear and well organized, contains content that is accurate, appropriate to the audience and purpose, and is complete. Provide a solution that contains no errors in spelling, grammar, or style.	Construct a solution in which some components are unclear, poorly organized, inconsistent, or incomplete. Misjudge the needs of the audience. Have some errors in spelling, grammar, or style, but the errors do not detract from comprehension.	Construct a solution that is unclear, incomplete, or poorly organized; contains some inaccurate or inappropriate content; and contains many errors in spelling, grammar, or style. Do not solve the problem.
3-Format & Layout	Format and arrange all elements to communicate information and ideas, clarify function, illustrate relationships, and indicate relative importance.	Apply appropriate format and layout features to some elements, but not others. Overuse features, causing minor distraction.	Apply format and layout that does not communicate information or ideas clearly. Do not use format and layout features to clarify function, illustrate relationships, or indicate relative importance. Use available features excessively, causing distraction.
4-Process	Use an organized approach that integrates planning, development, self-assessment, revision, and reflection.	Demonstrate an organized approach in some areas, but not others; or, use an insufficient process of organization throughout.	Do not use an organized approach to solve the problem.

OUTCOMES-BASED ASSESSMENTS

Problem Solving Project 1G Help Desk

In this project, you will construct a solution by applying any combination of the skills you practiced from the Objectives in Projects 1A and 1B.

For Project 1G, you will need the following file:

ie01_1G_Help_Desk

You will save your document as:

Lastname_Firstname_1G_Help_Desk

From the student files that accompany this textbook, open the **Chapter_Files** folder, and then in **Chapter_01** folder, locate and open the Word document **ie01_1G_Help_Desk**. Save the document in your chapter folder as **Lastname_Firstname_1G_Help_Desk**

The following email question has arrived at the Help Desk from an employee at the Bell Orchid Hotels' corporate office. In the Word form, construct a response based on your knowledge of Windows 8. Although an email response is not as formal as a letter, you should still use good grammar, good sentence structure, professional language, and a polite tone. Save your document and submit the response as directed by your instructor.

To: Help Desk

I have asked my research assistant to conduct some Internet research about what hotels around the country are doing in regard to designing innovative restaurants. Is there a way he could organize the sites he wants me to review by geographic location and by type of restaurant?

END | You have completed Project 1G

OUTCOMES-BASED ASSESSMENTS

Problem Solving   Project 1H Help Desk

In this project, you will construct a solution by applying any combination of the skills you practiced from the Objectives in Projects 1A and 1B.

For Project 1H, you will need the following file:

ie01_1H_Help_Desk

You will save your document as:

Lastname_Firstname_1H_Help_Desk

From the student files that accompany this textbook, open the **Chapter_Files** folder, and then in the **Chapter_01** folder, locate and open **ie01_1H_Help_Desk**. Save the document in your chapter folder as **Lastname_Firstname_1H_Help_Desk**

The following email question has arrived at the Help Desk from an employee at the Bell Orchid Hotels' corporate office. In the Word form, construct a response based on your knowledge of Windows 8. Although an email response is not as formal as a letter, you should still use good grammar, good sentence structure, professional language, and a polite tone. Save your document and submit the response as directed by your instructor.

To: Help Desk

Guests who use the computers in our hotel Business Centers have inquired about how they can prevent others from seeing the sites they visited and potentially seeing personal information. What instructions could we post at each of these computers to advise guests how to remove any such information from these public computers?

END | You have completed Project 1H

OUTCOMES-BASED ASSESSMENTS

Problem Solving   Project 1I Help Desk

In this project, you will construct a solution by applying any combination of the skills you practiced from the Objectives in Projects 1A and 1B.

For Project 1I, you will need the following file:

ie01_1I_Help_Desk

You will save your document as:

Lastname_Firstname_1I_Help_Desk

From the student files that accompany this textbook, open the **Chapter_Documents** folder, and then open the Word form **ie01_1I_Help_Desk**. Save the document in your chapter folder as **Lastname_Firstname_1I_Help_Desk**

The following email question has arrived at the Help Desk from an employee at the Bell Orchid Hotels' corporate office. In the Word document, construct a response based on your knowledge of Windows 8. Although an email response is not as formal as a letter, you should still use good grammar, good sentence structure, professional language, and a polite tone. Save your document and submit the response as directed by your instructor.

To: Help Desk

Guests commonly stop by the Front Desk at our hotels and inquire about what the weather will be like in the next few days. Is there a way we could have something on all of the Front Desk computers that would provide the Desk Clerks with constantly updated weather information?

> **END | You have completed Project 1I**

Index

P

Page Setup dialog box, 29–30
page tools/App available button, 5, 7
phishing, 35, 38
pin site button, 5
plug-ins, 19, 38
Pop-Up Blocker, 33–34, 38
Pop-up Blocker Settings dialog box, 33
pop-ups, 33, 38
portals, 28, 38
Print dialog box, 29–31
Print Preview window, IE, 28–29
printing webpages, 14, 28–31
protected mode, 34, 38
protecting data, 33–35
protocol prefix, 6, 38

Q-R

redisplay address bar, 8
refresh button, 5
review and assessment guides, 37
roaming feature, 6
rubrics, 47

S

Save Webpage dialog box, 32
saving webpage information, 32–33
screen parts, IE 10, 5, 20

search

Internet, 12–14
social results, 12–13, 38
search engines
Bing, social results, 12–13, 38
defined, 38
search providers, 12, 36, 38
search providers, 12, 36, 38
Settings charm, 7, 16 shortcuts, keyboard,
8, 10. *See also* icons
site icon, 5, 20
skills assessments, 39–42
SmartScreen Filter, 35, 38
social results, 12–13, 38
sponsored links, 12–13, 38
stylus pen, 3
surfing, 3, 38. *See also* browsing
synchronize, roaming feature, 6

T

tabbed browsing, 8–12, 19–21, 38
tabs
cycling through, 23
IE navigation, 8–12
Tabs bar, 9–10, 38
temporary Internet files,
14–15, 38
text size, webpages, 31
top level domains (TLDs), 6, 38

U

URLs (Uniform Resource Locators),
definition, 4, 38
user accounts, roaming
feature, 6

V

viewing browsing history, 27

W

web browsers. *See* browsers
web logs, 3, 38
webpages
emailing, 33
printing, 14, 28–31
Save Webpage dialog box, 32
saving information, 32–33
text size, 31
windows
browsing, 5, 7–11, 38
IE Print Preview window, 28–29
pop-up, 33, 38
Windows Defender, 34, 38
Windows Help and Support, 35

X-Z

zoom, IE 10, 31